Student Speeches Video Guide

Public Speaking

Student Speeches Video Guide

Public Speaking

FOURTH EDITION

Michael Osborn
University of Memphis

Suzanne Osborn
University of Memphis

HOUGHTON MIFFLIN COMPANY   BOSTON   NEW YORK

Sponsoring Editor: George T. Hoffman
Editorial Assistant: Kara Maltzahn
Senior Manufacturing Coordinator: Marie Barnes
Marketing Manager: Pamela J. Laskey

Printed in the U.S.A.

ISBN: 0-395-80885-5

123456789-VG-00 99 98 97 96

Contents

Introduction to the Video Guide

When we first began teaching public speaking over three decades ago, we often wished that we had speeches available on film to help students learn essential skills of performance and criticism. We would have welcomed the new videotape provided by the Houghton Mifflin Company to accompany the fourth edition of *Public Speaking*.

The videotape includes sixteen self-introductory, informative, and persuasive classroom speeches. These speeches range in quality from below average to excellent. While a few of them are quite good, all of them contain interesting problems and some are deeply flawed. Students should be able to learn from the speeches' successes and their mistakes.

For each student speech we provide four types of material: (1) a transcript of the speech, (2) an evaluation sheet summarizing how we assess it, (3) a discussion guide that raises questions about the speech, and (4) a commentary that indicates how we would respond to these questions. Feel free to copy and distribute these materials in your classes.

Before beginning a round of speeches, select appropriate speeches from this videotape to show in class. Frame discussion questions for each speech, using the guide we provide and your own questions pertinent to the emphasis you want to achieve. Consider whether you want to distribute these questions before or after students watch the speeches. Listing them before the speech results in more focused, directed viewing by students. Listing them after the speech is nondirective and may produce more creative observations. Use the commentary we provide to prompt and enrich the discussion. The more the students make useful discoveries as they watch the speeches, the better. We fully expect (and hope!) that there may be argument and even disagreement with us and within the class during these discussions. There is always something new to discover about speech texts.

In addition to this videotape, be sure to ask your Houghton Mifflin representative about other teaching resources made available to help users of *Public Speaking*.

We are grateful to Professors Katherine Hendrix, David Liban, and Brooke Quigley of the University of Memphis, whose hard work made this videotape possible. We also appreciate the efforts of numerous teachers of the basic course at Memphis for helping us find the speeches. And, of course, we are especially grateful to the students who were willing to expose all the rhetorical warts and blemishes, as well as excellences, of their first speeches to a critical world. We continue to be grateful to John Bakke, chair of the Department of Communication at the University of Memphis, who encouraged this project, and to Richard Ranta, dean of the College of Communication and Fine Arts at the University, who made available its superb televisual facilities. Such friends are a rare and incredible blessing.

Michael Osborn
Suzanne Osborn

Student Speeches Video Guide

Public Speaking

SPEECHES OF SELF-INTRODUCTION

My Secret Passion

Elizabeth Anne Douglas

I am very grateful this afternoon to have the opportunity to share with you a secret desire of mine. So secret is it in fact that even my close friends don't know. Most of my family members don't know either. I am very happy to be able to share it with you and to publicly declare what has for so long been an unspoken aspiration. And I am very appreciative to be able to do it in front of such welcoming faces. That does make it easier.

Before I can tell you this, dare I say, passion that I have kept hidden for so long, there is something I have to let you know about myself. I'm right handed. My secret desire then is to be more proficient with the use of my left hand. Now I know some might say that that's a pretty silly thing to have as a goal, but maybe if I can tell you how it all started, you might understand.

My mother used to share with me the most beautiful stories about her Aunt Althea. She was ambidextrous. My mother would go over to her house and visit her and Aunt Althea would be writing a letter. She would start off with her right hand and when the task got too tedious, she would just pop that pen in her left hand and continue writing. And the writing would be of the same quality and she would write with the same speed as she had with her right hand. My mother recalls sitting next to her on the front porch and just looking up to her as she was doing her needle work. "Aunt Athelia, switch hands," she would beg. It was a fascination with my mom, but for me, it's an aspiration.

When I was in high school, like my senior year, I suddenly realized that I had begun to meet a lot of the goals that I had set for myself. Academically and socially, I was turning out to be the kind of person I had hoped I would be and it began to uh, wonder in my mind, why I left this one goal on the backburner. Why not continue to pursue this goal too? It was the second semester of my senior year that I started to wear my watch on my right hand, the way a lot of left-handed people do. Kind of a talisman to spirit me on if ever I got discouraged about using my right hand too much. And maybe a silent proclamation to the rest of the world that hey! Elizabeth is doing something a little bit different. And I have actually made some accomplishments, some strides, in this, this my goal. I've noticed that, rather unconsciously, I'll reach for doors, to open them with my left hand or reach for my dinner glass with my left hand. And one of the biggest things is that I'm now able to peel an orange—not using a knife, I am not yet trusting sharp objects in my left hand—but peel an orange with great big peels and just have the fruit ready to eat when I'm done with it. It's very satisfying. The best thing though that I can do with my left hand, I am a whiz at the remote control operation.

Are there any left-handed people here? No? Do you know any? Are they not admirable folks? They have so much to put up with. I know that you might think that it is silly to admire somebody just because they have something that is innate, something they couldn't choose. But this is really a right-handed world. When you go to a water fountain—you may not think about it because we're all right handed—but when we reach for the spout, it's on that side. Left handed people either have to reach over or use a hand they are not more comfortable with. And try cutting a straight line with a pair of scissors that weren't made for your fingers. It's got to be difficult. And that's one thing that I would like to ask of all of us today, that when we look at left-handed people, we realize the kind of things they have to go through. The world just wasn't made for them. The next time you take notes using a composition notebook, be grateful that your arm isn't getting the creases from the wire spiral and that you're not smearing the ink on the page.

Something else too I'd like to ask you, to be encouraging of people in whatever their goals are—no matter how nonsensical you think they are or how silly it is to even pursue it. If you see that person making strides in that goal, encourage that person on. Because it really does mean a lot. And if you catch me on the street, picking up litter with my left hand, don't just applaud my act towards the environment, but say, "Way to go, Elizabeth, for picking that up with your left hand and not your right." It really does mean a lot, and I'd appreciate it. Thank you!

SPEECH EVALUATION FORM

SPEAKER Elizabeth Anne Douglas   **TOPIC** "My Secret Passion"   **DATE** _____

Overall Considerations

__5__	Did the speaker seem committed to the topic?
__4__	Did the speech meet the requirements of the assignment?
__5__	Was the speech adapted to fit the audience?
__5__	Did the speech promote identification among topic, audience, and speaker?
__3__	Was the purpose of the speech clear?
__5__	Was the topic handled with imagination and freshness?
__5__	Did the speech meet high ethical standards?

Substance

__4__	Was the topic worthwhile?
__NA__	Had the speaker done sufficient research?
__NA__	Were the main ideas supported with reliable and relevant information?
__NA__	Was testimony used appropriately?
__NA__	Were the sources documented appropriately?
__5__	Were examples or narratives used effectively?
__NA__	Was the reasoning clear and correct?

Structure

__5__	Did the introduction spark your interest?
__4__	Did the introduction adequately preview the message?
__5__	Was the speech easy to follow?
__3__	Could you identify the main points of the speech?
__5__	Were transitions used to tie the speech together?
__4__	Did the conclusion summarize the message?
__4__	Did the conclusion help you remember the speech?

Presentation

__5__	Was the language clear, simple, and direct?
__5__	Was the language colorful?
__5__	Were grammar and pronunciations correct?
__5+__	Was the speech presented extemporaneously?
__5__	Were notes used unobtrusively?
__5__	Was the speaker appropriately enthusiastic?
__5__	Did the speaker maintain good eye contact?
__5__	Did gestures and body language complement ideas?
__5__	Was the speaker's voice expressive?
__5__	Were the rate and loudness appropriate to the material?
__5__	Did the speaker uses pauses appropriately?
__NA__	Did presentation aids make the message clearer or more memorable?
__NA__	Were presentation aids skillfully integrated into the speech?
__5__	Was the presentation free from distracting mannerisms?

Discussion Guide for "My Secret Passion"

1. In terms of the self-awareness inventory, which approach to the self-introductory speech does Elizabeth Douglas choose?

2. Which of the four qualities of ethos discussed in Chapter 2 does the speech develop?

3. We regard this speech as an "exemplary model of extemporaneous presentation." What does Elizabeth do to earn this evaluation?

4. How and how well does this speech make use of narrative as a form of supporting material?

Commentary on "My Secret Passion"

The function of the self-introductory speech is to depict oneself in a manner that will help later speech efforts. In her self-introductory speech, Elizabeth Anne Douglas takes a considerable risk. She chooses to introduce herself by describing a life-goal, her "secret passion," an approach that might have produced a quite serious, if not daring, speech. Instead, Elizabeth offers what might be construed as a gentle caricature of the "reveal-all," confessional approach to self-introduction made popular by tabloid television interview shows. She takes what might have been a trivial subject and transforms it into a charming speech that reveals her as a thoroughly likable, poised, confident, and competent person. In Chapter 2 of our textbook, we describe the "likable" speaker as one who "seems to radiate goodness and good will and inspires audience affection in return." That pretty well describes the Elizabeth we see revealed in this speech.

Her speech, which we assessed as an "A" effort, offers an exemplary model of extemporaneous presentation. Her face and gestures are fully expressive and engaging as she establishes a warm, confiding relationship with her listeners. When she describes her Aunt Althea's "gift" of ambidexterity, she reveals her mastery of narrative technique as well. She shows how to make characters and scenes come alive through active, colorful language, and she shows how to build suspense as she tells a story. While her tribute to left-handed people has a mock-serious quality, "Are they not admirable folks? The world just wasn't made for them," she takes her speech onto a more serious level as she urges tolerance and even encouragement for each other's secret goals, even if these should seem "nonsensical."

Perhaps the ultimate test of a self-introductory speech is whether listeners look forward to later speeches. The only problem with doing so well on a first speech is that one establishes extremely high expectations. With this speech Elizabeth challenged herself to a significant growth experience during her public speaking class.

Who's Going to Stand?

Valesa Johnson

Unethical. Dishonest. Underhanded. Corrupt. Fraudulent. Crooks. These are just a few of the adjectives that have been used to describe lawyers. So why would anyone in his or her right mind want to become a part of such a disrespected profession? How about the acquittal of known murderers or how about the ill-fated convictions of the innocent? Better yet, how about each and every individual entangled in this city's justice system that is incarcerated and not being rehabilitated?

It seems to me that true justice for each of these is more than reason enough to enter an otherwise questionable profession. Rob Bryant and J. W. Milam were allowed to walk out of an American courtroom despite the fact that everyone in this country knew that they had brutally and senselessly murdered a fourteen-year-old boy whose name I shouldn't have to mention. Or how about a Florida man who was released from a state prison after spending ten years of his life on death row because the state finally realized or finally admitted that they had prosecuted and convicted the wrong individual?

I know you may think that these incidents are isolated, ancient, or too far from home to be concerned about. But I say you're wrong. If you took a notion to go down to 201 Poplar at nine o'clock in the morning on any weekday, you will find yourself faced with hundreds of individuals and their quest for justice. Many of these will be convicted and rightly so. Unfortunately, while they're incarcerated, the illiterate and unlearned will remain so as will the unskilled and the uncrafted. Who's going to stand for these so that they have an alternative to standing in the revolving doors of the criminal justice complex? Or better yet, how about the ones that are truly innocent? Oh yes, that's right, not everyone in the court system, not everyone institutionalized, is guilty. Who is going to stand for these?

I will. And I know you're asking yourselves, what's going to make me any different from the rest of the skum attorneys? Well, let me ask you a question. Have you ever stood accused and were devoid of any wrong doing? Have you ever had to stand idly by and listen to a prosecuting attorney, who couldn't even pronounce your first name, try to encourage people who had known you for years into assassinating your character? Not because he or she had evidence that pointed to your guilt, simply to add another notch to the belt of conviction? Have you ever paid an attorney handsomely to work on your behalf to have him allow the states to keep you entangled in their system even though he knew they had no case against you, but he also knew that every time your name appeared on that docket his pockets got fatter? Have you ever spent two years of your life seeking vindication for a charge that never should have been laid to your claim? If you can answer yes to any of these questions then you know what makes me different. Unjustified acquittals, erroneous convictions, and those institutionalized with no hope for a better life. These are the reasons, but who's going to stand?

You know, we were once blessed with a true advocate for justice, attorney Barbara Jordan. She fought a long, hard battle to ensure that we all abided by the constitutional creed, "All men are created equal" and "justice for all." Someone has to continue to beat the path of justice for all men. That includes black men, white men, yellow men, brown men and *women*. Someone has got to continue to fight the good fight. And I submit to you today that I am that someone.

SPEECH EVALUATION FORM

SPEAKER Valesa Johnson   **TOPIC** "Who's Going to Stand?"   **DATE** _____

Overall Considerations

5+	Did the speaker seem committed to the topic?
5	Did the speech meet the requirements of the assignment?
4	Was the speech adapted to fit the audience?
5	Did the speech promote identification among topic, audience, and speaker?
4	Was the purpose of the speech clear?
5	Was the topic handled with imagination and freshness?
5	Did the speech meet high ethical standards?

Substance

5	Was the topic worthwhile?
NA	Had the speaker done sufficient research?
NA	Were the main ideas supported with reliable and relevant information?
NA	Was testimony used appropriately?
3	Were the sources documented appropriately?
4	Were examples or narratives used effectively?
5	Was the reasoning clear and correct?

Structure

5	Did the introduction spark your interest?
4	Did the introduction adequately preview the message?
4	Was the speech easy to follow?
4	Could you identify the main points of the speech?
4	Were transitions used to tie the speech together?
4	Did the conclusion summarize the message?
5	Did the conclusion help you remember the speech?

Presentation

5	Was the language clear, simple, and direct?
5	Was the language colorful?
4	Were grammar and pronunciations correct?
5	Was the speech presented extemporaneously?
5	Were notes used unobtrusively?
5	Was the speaker appropriately enthusiastic?
5	Did the speaker maintain good eye contact?
5	Did gestures and body language complement ideas?
5+	Was the speaker's voice expressive?
5	Were the rate and loudness appropriate to the material?
5	Did the speaker uses pauses appropriately?
NA	Did presentation aids make the message clearer or more memorable?
NA	Were presentation aids skillfully integrated into the speech?
5	Was the presentation free from distracting mannerisms?

Discussion Guide for "Who's Going to Stand?"

1. Which qualities of personal ethos does Valesa's speech emphasize?

2. Which probe questions in the self-awareness inventory might have prompted this speech?

3. What are the special strengths of this speech?

4. How might the speech have been improved?

Commentary on "Who's Going to Stand?"

The virtues of Valesa Johnson's self-introductory speech complement very nicely those we observed in Elizabeth Anne Douglas's speech. While Elizabeth's speech emphasized the likableness and competence dimensions of ethos, Valesa's speech stresses qualities of character and forcefulness. While Elizabeth takes a lighthearted approach to goals as the defining feature of her life, Valesa is deadly serious in her use of that theme. Especially noteworthy are the commitment and passion communicated by this speech. When Valesa answers her own refrain, "who's going to stand?" with her assertion, "I will," no one doubts that she will indeed take an uncompromising stand in her life on behalf of the values she sees endangered in contemporary legal practices. Her manner may be somewhat confrontational and she may overuse rhetorical questions, but she anticipates well possible audience reactions and responds to them. Her expressive voice conveys her conviction and strength of character. We can certainly see the influence of Barbara Jordan as the role model in her life. By her presentation style she bears personal witness to and validates her admiration for Jordan.

Every good speech can always be better. Valesa's introduction is striking, but she might have made a better adaptation at the beginning to her student audience. She concludes her speech rather abruptly. In the body of her speech, she needed to document her examples more carefully. This is a persistent problem in student speeches, perhaps because students may notice that speakers in public life often do not document the sources of their information. But such speakers often enjoy considerable authority because of their age and position, so they may need less documentation to make their assertions credible for many listeners. Student speakers, who usually lack such authority, require more documentation to support what they say.

Despite these possible flaws, we evaluate this speech as an "A" effort largely because of its commitment and conviction and the freshness and vigor of its statement.

The Notes of My Life

Kevin Howse

Being as this is an oral presentation and knowing how I hate to talk in front of people, I figure that the only way I will survive up here will be if I relate this to something I know how to do. Therefore, I am going to relate this to playing the piano. Uh, my life consists of a B flat, G, C, and F. This is a minor chord.

Okay, now you're probably wondering where the B flat kicks in. All right, the B flat is for my home town. I come from Humboldt, Tennessee. Now the B flat kicks in with the Humboldt because they call Humboldt the town the boat that doesn't float. So uh, that's where the B comes in with the B flat. Now I am from a small neighborhood town and I am a neighborly person as a result of this town. Now the biggest event we have in this town is called the Strawberry Festival. Now everyone lives for the Strawberry Festival, it's like the biggest event of the whole year. Now I feel like my town contributed to my character because like I said I am a neighborly person as a result of this town. I know everyone and if I'm walking down the street, I'm probably going to run into my cousin, or my father, or my sister. That's just how small the town is.

Now the G part of my life is the graduation. Like everyone else I'm sure you thought you knew everything when you graduated. I was only seventeen-years-old and I did graduate in the top percent of my class. But I feel like this was a hindrance rather than an attribute because like I said I graduated in the top percent of my class and the majority of my friends barely made it through by a point or two. So I feel like I had a big head as a result of this and I felt like jobs would just be offered to me, you know, because I did graduate in the top percent. But this would soon show me that that was not the road that I was going to be going on.

Now the C part of my life was the college life. And here at the University of Memphis I am a junior and a Manufacturing/Engineering Technology major. I am in the marching band, I am in the varsity band, I am in a Greek organization, and I am a member of the Society of Manufacturing Engineers. And that's all good and dandy, but when I first got here I had no idea that I would be in all of these. I was actually terrified when I first got here and that was a result of the B flat and the G. B flat, like I said I am from a small town and when I got here at college I wasn't used to speaking to someone and they didn't speak back to me. And uh, the G, the graduation, I graduated from the top percent of my class and when I got here in school I felt like I could just breeze through like I did in high-school, but, heh, that wasn't it. I had to study so the B flat and the G ties into the C and you can start seeing how this chord is kicking in together.

Now when I get to the last note you can tell how this chord is going to blend in and sound wonderful. Now the F part of my life is the family life and I feel like this is the most important note. I come from a small family uh, my mother, she's young, my father, he's young and my sister, she's a freshman at Austin Peay University. Now not to be kicking anyone else aside, but I feel like the most important influential part of this family would be my father. My father, he comes from a family of twelve, a large family, and he had to work for everything he had. And he is a well-respected man in the community. No one has anything bad to say about him and that's how I want to be when I get established.

Now, uh, in conclusion, these notes are just plain notes by themselves and you all probably wouldn't be able to tell them apart, but when you put them all together they make up a good and consistent harmony and chord, just like my life. When I put these aspects of my life together they make up who I am.

SPEECH EVALUATION FORM

SPEAKER Kevin Howse _____ **TOPIC** "The Notes of My Life" _____ **DATE** _____

Overall Considerations

4	Did the speaker seem committed to the topic?
5	Did the speech meet the requirements of the assignment?
4	Was the speech adapted to fit the audience?
4	Did the speech promote identification among topic, audience, and speaker?
3	Was the purpose of the speech clear?
5	Was the topic handled with imagination and freshness?
5	Did the speech meet high ethical standards?

Substance

5	Was the topic worthwhile?
NA	Had the speaker done sufficient research?
NA	Were the main ideas supported with reliable and relevant information?
NA	Was testimony used appropriately?
NA	Were the sources documented appropriately?
3	Were examples or narratives used effectively?
NA	Was the reasoning clear and correct?

Structure

4	Did the introduction spark your interest?
3	Did the introduction adequately preview the message?
4	Was the speech easy to follow?
4	Could you identify the main points of the speech?
4	Were transitions used to tie the speech together?
4	Did the conclusion summarize the message?
4	Did the conclusion help you remember the speech?

Presentation

4	Was the language clear, simple, and direct?
4	Was the language colorful?
5	Were grammar and pronunciations correct?
4	Was the speech presented extemporaneously?
4	Were notes used unobtrusively?
4	Was the speaker appropriately enthusiastic?
4	Did the speaker maintain good eye contact?
3	Did gestures and body language complement ideas?
4	Was the speaker's voice expressive?
4	Were the rate and loudness appropriate to the material?
3	Did the speaker uses pauses appropriately?
NA	Did presentation aids make the message clearer or more memorable?
NA	Were presentation aids skillfully integrated into the speech?
3	Was the presentation free from distracting mannerisms?

Discussion Guide for "The Notes of My Life"

1. Which themes in the self-awareness inventory does Kevin explore in his speech?

2. The central conception of Kevin's speech is expressed in a metaphor. Identify this metaphor, and discuss its strengths and limitations as a pattern for the development of the speech.

3. You have been assigned to coach Kevin on presentation skills for his next speech. How would you go about your assignment?

4. Evaluate Kevin's use of supporting materials.

Commentary on "The Notes of My Life"

We continue to be amazed at the creativity of students as they develop self-introductory speeches using the self-awareness inventory developed in Chapter 2. As Kevin Howse pondered the various probe questions there, he had a moment of inspiration. It occured to him that the major themes of his life might be expressed as a musical chord combining the B flat, G, C, and F notes. The fact that this is a harmonious chord suggests Kevin's positive feelings about his life and his impression that his experiences have enriched each other and formed a coherent identity.

Developing his speech in terms of this innovative metaphor allowed Kevin to interweave his hometown background, his high school experiences, college experiences, and family. He did need to develop more effective transitions as he moved from point to point. He overworked "now" as a connective between points and even sentences. As he added supporting material to this structure, Kevin needed to make more of his examples, to tell us more about the Strawberry Festival, or about his much respected father. Some well-chosen stories about both father and festival would have brought these examples to life and enriched the speech.

Presenting this speech in front of cameras was clearly not comfortable for Kevin. He needs to work on some presentation problems. His oral grammar and enunciation patterns leave much to be desired, and he has an unfortunate tendency to bounce from side to side as he presents his speech.

Perhaps the most interesting feature of Kevin's speech is how it demonstrates the vital role of the listener in completing the meaning structure of speeches. Suzanne and Michael, as they screened this speech, had quite different reactions to the structural conception underlying the speech. Michael thought it was clever but somewhat obscure, finding the development of the speech difficult to follow. Suzanne had no problem at all tracking the unfolding pattern of the speech. As we reflected on this difference, it suddenly occurred to us that we brought quite different backgrounds to the role of listener. Suzanne, who had had musical training, was a competent listener for the speech. Michael, without musical training, was not as well prepared to listen. While both thought the speech merited a low "B" grade, Suzanne was better able to appreciate Kevin's work and gave it a more favorable evaluation.

As you show and discuss this speech in class, you might explore this notion of the competent listener and perhaps illustrate the importance of constructive listening to the success of a speech. First, have class members offer their evaluations and suggest a grade for this speech. Then divide the class into those with and without a background of musical training. See if the two groups differed in the ways they evaluated and graded the speech, and discuss the meanings of the results in class.

One Day a Week

Julie Cunningham

As I was preparing my speech for today I was thinking about things that I could tell you that would introduce myself in a good way. And I could have told you things that happened to me ten years ago or two years ago or even last week. But I decided to share something with you that I do once a week that's really changing and shaping my life in a good way.

Every Sunday morning before sunrise I arrive out at Shelby Forest State Park with a couple of friends of mine and when I get out there my responsibilities include gathering wood and sweeping the area for the sweat lodge that I attend. Now a sweat lodge is a Native American ceremony of spirituality and purification and the lodge itself represents the womb of mother earth. And the idea is, you crawl in and pay your respects in the lodge and when you crawl out you are reborn to this world. This is a time of respect and prayer and singing as well as remembering our ancestors and sharing in each other's joy and sorrow and laughter and tears. I'd like to read a quote to you all from a book called *Turtle Island Alphabet* by Gerald Hausman.

> A mother by definition is one who gives birth to and cares for her children. Thus the Indian concept of the nurturing source of all good comes from within, not from without, the fecundity of maternal earth. This is a spiritual rather than a material relationship. You do not take from the mother, she gives freely to those whose reverence is declared by familial responsibility. Sonhood and daughterhood are rewarded with nourishment and love.

And the more time I spend out in these forests the more I am coming to realize the working relationship between mother earth and all of her children. This is a time when it is appropriate and welcomed for me to slow down and relax and take my time, and remembering things that are important to me in the past, present, and things that I am hoping for in the future. It's also a time for me to exist as one part of the whole and commune with all of my surroundings and relatives including my tree brothers and the four leggeds, the winged animals as well as some of my favorite people that I get to spend time with. These people are good for me in that I know them on a personal relationship but they uh, they enable me to be myself, and they call in this perfect serenity that surrounds us for the entire day. And while I'm out there I get the enjoyment of listening to the wind and feeling the warm sun on my face. And I feel so immune to the outside world where I'm back taking tests and studying and gossiping with friends. And when I'm out there, there is really no hurry at all for me to get back to this world.

And as I close I'd like to share with you a thought from Leonard Peltier, who was a Sioux elder and is in prison right now. This was a quote from a commencement speech he gave at a college graduation in 1993.

> And the light is getting brighter and brighter. I feel in my heart that now is the beginning of a true time for healing between our nations. Now perhaps we will be able to learn about and respect each other. We are in this together, my friends, the rich and poor, the red, white, black, brown and yellow. We share a responsibility for mother earth and all of those things that live and breathe upon her. Never forget that.

SPEECH EVALUATION FORM

SPEAKER Julie Cunningham   **TOPIC** "One Day a Week"   **DATE** _____

Overall Considerations

5	Did the speaker seem committed to the topic?
5	Did the speech meet the requirements of the assignment?
4	Was the speech adapted to fit the audience?
5	Did the speech promote identification among topic, audience, and speaker?
5	Was the purpose of the speech clear?
5	Was the topic handled with imagination and freshness?
5	Did the speech meet high ethical standards?

Substance

5	Was the topic worthwhile?
NA	Had the speaker done sufficient research?
NA	Were the main ideas supported with reliable and relevant information?
5	Was testimony used appropriately?
5	Were the sources documented appropriately?
5	Were examples or narratives used effectively?
NA	Was the reasoning clear and correct?

Structure

2	Did the introduction spark your interest?
3	Did the introduction adequately preview the message?
5	Was the speech easy to follow?
4	Could you identify the main points of the speech?
4	Were transitions used to tie the speech together?
4	Did the conclusion summarize the message?
5	Did the conclusion help you remember the speech?

Presentation

5	Was the language clear, simple, and direct?
5	Was the language colorful?
5	Were grammar and pronunciations correct?
5	Was the speech presented extemporaneously?
4	Were notes used unobtrusively?
5	Was the speaker appropriately enthusiastic?
5	Did the speaker maintain good eye contact?
5	Did gestures and body language complement ideas?
5	Was the speaker's voice expressive?
5	Were the rate and loudness appropriate to the material?
4	Did the speaker uses pauses appropriately?
NA	Did presentation aids make the message clearer or more memorable?
NA	Were presentation aids skillfully integrated into the speech?
5	Was the presentation free from distracting mannerisms?

Discussion Guide for "One Day a Week"

1. In terms of the self-awareness inventory, which probe question proved most useful to Julie? Why was it useful?

2. What purposes do you detect in Julie's speech? How well does she accomplish them?

3. Which forms of supporting material does Julie rely on?

4. How effectively does she use language? Which of her images do you remember, and why do you remember them?

5. What strengths would you advise Julie to build on in subsequent speeches? Which weaknesses should she work to improve?

Commentary on "One Day a Week"

As she reflected upon her self-awareness inventory, Julie Cunningham discovered that an unusual *activity*—her weekly participation in a sweat-lodge ritual—expressed the most distinctive things about herself. By discussing this ritual, she would be able to suggest her values and share her love for nature and her admiration for the ideals of Native Americans. The speech she constructs registers well on many of the dimensions of ethos, reflecting her as an imaginative, likable person with a strong character and sensitive intelligence. To the extent that she met the challenge of communicating her thoughts in effective oral presentation, she reinforced this image of herself as a competent person as well.

A less sympathetic evaluation of Julie's speech might argue that her very unconventionality is itself quite orthodox among those who sentimentalize Native Americans. Such critics, we think, would miss her point, which is to communicate a fresh sense of our identification with all life by sharing with us the adventures of her senses. By connecting us symbolically with her sensory experiences, she recharges our own awareness of, and obligation to, the natural world of which we are part.

The weakest part of Julie's speech comes at the beginning. As she proceeds, the speech seems to grow, and she emerges as a more effective communicator. More than any speech we have seen to this point, she knows how to use testimony effectively and how to document her sources. Thus she seems both knowledgeable and well-prepared, and she implies a compliment to her listeners as well—she takes both them and her ideals seriously. Moreover, her use of language is vivid, resulting in striking images that linger in the mind.

All in all, we think that Julie offers a graphic portrayal of her sweat lodge experience and in the process sketches an effective portrait of herself. We would assess this speech as an "A" effort.

A Child in the Mirror (Take 1)

Marquez Rhyne

Thank you for inviting me this morning. I am glad that I get the chance to introduce myself to you today. My name is Marquez Rhyne.

This morning I was getting myself together and wondering if I was looking presentable and I couldn't help but to smile at myself in the mirror. It's not often that I was able to do that as a child. When I looked in the mirror as a child all I saw was black and illegitimate. But now I see beautiful, brown. I didn't see hindrance. I didn't see blocks to success to jobs. I held my head down momentarily, and I looked back up into big brown eyes. Lost and confused eyes.

At school the other children would talk about their parents. What they did in their careers and what they did together. And when it got around to me they would ask, "Well, why do you only have one parent?" Well I didn't know because I was only a child! I thought that my mother just had me, that was just the way it was. I was kind of ignorant to the fact that I had an absent father. He was never around when I grew up. So consequently I had a chunk of my history, hence a chunk of my understanding, missing. I'd look back into those eyes and I'd say, "I'm a bastard!" and I'd look away. Then I would look back slowly, more confidently, and I would say, "No! I'm not. I'm beautiful!"

When you see a child in the mirror, look at that child, be observant, wonder what he or she is doing. Encourage that child. Reassure that child that he or she is wonderful! That they can be successful if they put their mind to it. Let them know that images and types and labels are just that. Let them know that you care about them. You know that they are important so they know that they are important. And you'll be able to look at yourself in the mirror and smile.

SPEECH EVALUATION FORM

SPEAKER Marquez Rhyne   **TOPIC** "A Child in the Mirror" (1)   **DATE** _____

Overall Considerations

5	Did the speaker seem committed to the topic?
4	Did the speech meet the requirements of the assignment?
3	Was the speech adapted to fit the audience?
4	Did the speech promote identification among topic, audience, and speaker?
3	Was the purpose of the speech clear?
5	Was the topic handled with imagination and freshness?
5	Did the speech meet high ethical standards?

Substance

5	Was the topic worthwhile?
NA	Had the speaker done sufficient research?
NA	Were the main ideas supported with reliable and relevant information?
NA	Was testimony used appropriately?
NA	Were the sources documented appropriately?
4	Were examples or narratives used effectively?
3	Was the reasoning clear and correct?

Structure

3	Did the introduction spark your interest?
4	Did the introduction adequately preview the message?
4	Was the speech easy to follow?
4	Could you identify the main points of the speech?
4	Were transitions used to tie the speech together?
4	Did the conclusion summarize the message?
5	Did the conclusion help you remember the speech?

Presentation

5	Was the language clear, simple, and direct?
5	Was the language colorful?
5	Were grammar and pronunciations correct?
5	Was the speech presented extemporaneously?
5	Were notes used unobtrusively?
5	Was the speaker appropriately enthusiastic?
5	Did the speaker maintain good eye contact?
5	Did gestures and body language complement ideas?
5	Was the speaker's voice expressive?
5	Were the rate and loudness appropriate to the material?
5+	Did the speaker uses pauses appropriately?
NA	Did presentation aids make the message clearer or more memorable?
NA	Were presentation aids skillfully integrated into the speech?
5	Was the presentation free from distracting mannerisms?

Discussion Guide for "A Child in the Mirror" (1)

1. What are the themes of Marquez's speech?

2. What central technique does he employ?

3. What are the strengths and weaknesses of this presentation?

4. Do you think an audience would have been receptive to this speech? Why or why not?

Commentary on "A Child in the Mirror" (1)

Marquez Rhyne made two recordings of his speech, "A Child in the Mirror," for this videotape. During his first speech, Marquez focused on his struggle against two stigmas, his blackness and his illegitimacy. During the second recording, Marquez also mentioned another stigma, his bisexuality. We have included both versions of the speech in order to discuss the issues they raise. Here, however, we shall confine our remarks to his first presentation.

As he reflected upon his identity through the self-awareness inventory, Marquez found that he had been shaped—and scarred—by his cultural background, the environment in which he grew up, and by his day-to-day experience. His life was best described as confronting and overcoming the negative challenges produced by those factors.

To express this sense of struggle, Marquez focused on a common but important experience: what do we see when we look at ourselves in the mirror? His answer is that we see first what we are *led* to see. If that is a negative self-portrait, then we must struggle to see what we *want* to see. In his case, he was led to see himself in terms of his blackness and his illegitimacy. He had to struggle before he could see himself in a better way. Marquez concludes by turning the focus away from his own intense personal quest to the audience, inviting them to help children form more positive and constructive self-images.

Marquez's speech raises a profound question of how much self-disclosure is too much, especially in a public speech. The answer obviously relies a great deal on the listeners, and whether they are able to give the speech a sympathetic hearing. Once again we are reminded that a competent listener is necessary to complete successfully the meaning intended in a speech. But here the question of competence is not so much a matter of previous knowledge—whether, for example, we have a musical background—as it is previous enculturation. Are listeners sophisticated enough, and fair-minded enough, to really hear Marquez's message?

Marquez helps himself a great deal by presenting his speech with grace and strength. He obviously trusts his audience a great deal, even though he presumably does not know them well. This trust may itself invite a positive reaction from them. His opening is rather stilted and formal. When the message is as wrenching and self-disclosive as we see in this speech, speakers can sometimes soften its impact, and relieve the tension, by a little gentle humor. When audiences can chuckle with speakers, they draw closer to them, and perhaps are better prepared to make a difficult identification with them.

As the speech develops, it is sometimes not clear who is looking in the mirror, the younger or the older Marquez, the child or the man we see before us. Images must have internal consistency to be most effective. If listeners must work to decipher the order of thoughts, they become distracted from the speaker's message. We would assign this version of the speech a "B" grade.

A Child in the Mirror (Take 2)

Marquez Rhyne

Good morning. Thank you for inviting me this morning to introduce myself to you. My name is Marquez Rhyne.

You know, getting ready this morning I was looking at myself in the mirror and I could not help but to smile. I wasn't always able to do this. I remember being a child, feeling that all I saw in the mirror was blackness, negritude, illegitimacy. I didn't realize that I was actually beautiful, brown. I didn't see the hindrance to jobs and to success that everyone was telling me existed. Little did I know that it would come to me much later. I held my head down momentarily. Thoughts of negritude, fatherlessness, and sexual identity came up. I looked into big brown eyes, lost, confused eyes.

I remember all the other children would sit and discuss their parents and what their careers were and what they did together and when it got around to me they were asking, "Well, why do you only have one parent?" Well I didn't know, I was only a child! I figured my mother just had me. That I only had one parent. Little did I know that my father was absent. So a whole chunk of my history, a whole chunk of my understanding, was missing. I'd look in my eyes and say "I'm a bastard. I'm a sissy."

I knew I was different when I was growing up. Somehow I knew not to talk about it. I knew this was one thing you never discussed. It wasn't until years later that I realized that I was a bisexual. I can now talk confidently about this and look at myself in the mirror and say "No! I'm not a bastard. I am not illegitimate. I am beautiful, I am brown, and I am a strong man!"

When you see a child looking into the mirror, I implore you, encourage that child. Be an assurance to that child that they can be successful, regardless of the labels that are put upon them. Let them know that the labels are just that, they are labels. Let them walk away from the mirrors confident, secure, proud and I bet that you'll be able to look at yourselves in the mirror and smile at yourselves.

SPEECH EVALUATION FORM

SPEAKER Marquez Rhyne _____ **TOPIC** "A Child in the Mirror" (2) **DATE** _____

Overall Considerations

5	Did the speaker seem committed to the topic?
5	Did the speech meet the requirements of the assignment?
3	Was the speech adapted to fit the audience?
4	Did the speech promote identification among topic, audience, and speaker?
5	Was the purpose of the speech clear?
5	Was the topic handled with imagination and freshness?
5	Did the speech meet high ethical standards?

Substance

5	Was the topic worthwhile?
NA	Had the speaker done sufficient research?
NA	Were the main ideas supported with reliable and relevant information?
NA	Was testimony used appropriately?
NA	Were the sources documented appropriately?
4	Were examples or narratives used effectively?
4	Was the reasoning clear and correct?

Structure

3	Did the introduction spark your interest?
4	Did the introduction adequately preview the message?
5	Was the speech easy to follow?
5	Could you identify the main points of the speech?
4	Were transitions used to tie the speech together?
4	Did the conclusion summarize the message?
5	Did the conclusion help you remember the speech?

Presentation

5	Was the language clear, simple, and direct?
5	Was the language colorful?
5	Were grammar and pronunciations correct?
5+	Was the speech presented extemporaneously?
5	Were notes used unobtrusively?
5+	Was the speaker appropriately enthusiastic?
5	Did the speaker maintain good eye contact?
5	Did gestures and body language complement ideas?
5+	Was the speaker's voice expressive?
5	Were the rate and loudness appropriate to the material?
5	Did the speaker uses pauses appropriately?
NA	Did presentation aids make the message clearer or more memorable?
NA	Were presentation aids skillfully integrated into the speech?
5	Was the presentation free from distracting mannerisms?

Discussion Guide for "Child in the Mirror" (2)

1. Does Marquez go too far in this version in discussing his sexual orientation? What might be the impact on his ethos?

2. How important is presentation to the effectiveness of this speech?

Commentary on "A Child in the Mirror" (2)

Conventional wisdom (CW) would have it that Marquez violates unwritten rules of self-disclosure in this version of his speech. To the burden of negative stereotypes heaped upon him as a child, he now adds derogatory social attitudes towards his sexual orientation. If he is indeed introducing himself to an audience of strangers, doesn't he run a terrible risk by revealing himself so completely and intimately? Won't he embarrass or shock many listeners, and worse still, activate the very mindless stereotypes he wants to counter? CW would advise Marquez to concentrate more in this speech on building positive ethos with listeners, talking less directly about the self and more about accomplishments and aims that might reveal competence, character, and promise as a human being. Build your ethos, CW would counsel, so that listeners will give you a better hearing should you do decide in some later persuasive speech to indict the ignorance and intolerance of sexual "labels."

It's hard to dismiss easily such criticism and advice. Indeed, CW *is* CW because it is usually correct. On the other hand, we confess that we find this speech to be quite compelling and courageous. Of the two efforts, it may be less wise, but we think it is more effective. For one thing, it does paint the complete picture of a life that has struggled heroically to find the equipoise this speech exhibits. We agree that it would take a "strong man" to give this speech; in that sense it is self-validating. Therefore, we would argue with CW that the speech does build the ethos of character and strength. Moreover, Marquez seems likable and well-disposed to his listeners. He trusts them with this information, and his manner is both pleasant and respectful. The presentation of the speech is quite effective: Marquez does not hesitate or falter, and his own lack of embarrassment may help others get over theirs. Both voice and face are quite expressive and help him make his case.

All in all, we find this speech difficult to assess. But for its courage and quality, if not its wisdom, we regard this version as an "A" effort.

INFORMATIVE SPEECHES

Same Holidays, Different Customs

Stephanie Herrera

I know you all know that from my previous speech, my self-introduction speech, I am Hispanic: my mother is Mexican and my father is American. I know you all are from different backgrounds from your self-introduction speeches, and so I thought you might be interested in learning about Hispanic customs. Specifically, I thought I would talk about the difference between the Mexican customs of Christmas, weddings, the Day of the Dead, and coming-out customs as compared to American customs.

Christmas in Mexico is not really a gift-giving holiday. It's more of a religious observance. They have this parade, basically it's called a *posada*. It means "where they stop." They join at the church and then they go along the streets in this neighborhood—it's usually a designated route—go along the streets in this neighborhood caroling and stopping at different houses and caroling. And at the houses that they stop at and carol, they will be given gifts of food, usually cakes, small cakes or something. They go on, they pick one house months in advance to design a nativity scene. And the nativity scene can be quite elaborate or just the bare basics. My mother told me about once when her sister was chosen to have her house be the designated spot for the *posada* to stop. And her sister went all-out. She had completely an elaborate nativity scene. Not only did she have the nativity scene, but she had the whole journey from where the wise men started in the fields to the nativity scene. She brought in, she cleared out a whole room of her house and she brought in mountains. And she even had a little river coming down the mountain. She brought in trees and rocks and just the whole journey. It was like when you walked in her house it was like you were going on the journey with the three wise men to the nativity scene. The *posada,* basically they are trying to honor what they call *niño dios*. Instead of Santa Claus they have *niño dios*, which means "baby God" in English. And they get to the nativity scene and a huge party ensues. Everybody has been cooking for weeks. They have all kinds of food and drinks and music. And it's just a huge party. And they party until dawn. Basically, a party until the sun comes up, and then they all go home and they rest. Christmas Day for them, Christmas actual day, December 25th, is a day of rest for them. But that's not the end of their *posada*. The end of their *posada* comes on January the 6th. That's when, that is called the *Los Tres Reyes*, which means "the three kings." It is basically the same procession to the nativity scene to disassemble the scene and help the family clear out their house and clear out whatever nativity scene they have. And then they have another party—they party a lot.

Another custom that my mother told me about in Mexico that is quite similar to a custom that we have here in America is called *la dia de los muertos*, which means "the day of the dead." It is the equivalent of Halloween but it's celebrated on November the 1st. They don't give candy. Kid's don't go door-to-door. It does vary from region to region. Basically, the day of the dead for them is remembering the loved ones who've passed away. They'll get up early in the morning and their family will prepare their picnic, and they'll get lots of food again. And they'll get their garden tools and anything else they might need and they go to the cemeteries and clean up the graves of their loved ones. Or even if there is somebody who can't clean up a grave they'll go on and do it. And they just clean the cemetery, mow it, weed it, plant flowers, whatever's necessary. And then they break for lunch and they have a huge picnic. Just everybody who's there has a picnic. And then at dusk they go home and they have a huge feast in honor of their loved ones who have passed away. They set up— on a table—they set up pictures with candles and flowers to honor their loved ones and then they eat again.

Another thing that's quite similar to America is a coming-out party. In Mexico it's called *la quinceniera. La quinceniera* means "the fifteen-year-old princess." It is a coming-out party but it's celebrated on the fifteenth birthday, not the sixteenth birthday. It is the right of passion for a young Mexican girl to enter into society. She is not considered a woman until after her *quinceniera*. Some of the customs that they do on that, the girl will choose fourteen attendants who all wear formal gowns, all the same gown. It reminds me of bridesmaids because they're all the same gown and they're all formal and they're all dressed alike. And then the fifteen-year-old girl will very often, almost exclusively wear white. A white gown. And they all carry flowers and do that kind of thing. The attendants are usually family members but they also are friends. And they are usually between the ages of twelve and fourteen. The family will take the girl and the attendants to the church and she is formally presented in front of the congregation. "She is, this is our daughter and we are presenting you to her. This is her *la quinceniera* and she can now join society." They all go, the whole congregation goes back to the girl's family's house for a party. The girl has a white cake with fifteen layers and like a wedding cake. And like a wedding cake, I know some people here in the states will put tokens in their wedding cakes such as rings or ribbons or whatever to symbolize happiness in their future. For instance, at the *quinceniera* they will put a little ring in the cake to represent their hope for her finding a good marriage. And toasts are made and everyone dances and eats.

Some of the wedding customs were real interesting to me. I like their ideas a lot. First of all the groom's family pays for everything. The celebration begins three days earlier. It's a three-day barbecue where the bride and groom are the guests of honor and of course the groom's family pays for everything, the whole thing. On the third day the bride's family presents a token dowry to the groom's family. It's usually a bag of coins, not anything major. Just a few coins just to be a token of a dowry. The wedding is usually a Catholic Nuptial Mass because most Mexicans are by far Catholic. The priest will take what's called a *lasso*, and it is a rope, that is in the shape of a figure eight and it's tied in a knot in the middle. It's usually a white kind of lacy rope, it's real pretty and delicate. And what he'll do is he will take the rope and place one side over the groom's shoulders and then place the other side over the bride's shoulders and this is to symbolize them being bound together for the rest of their lives. Another custom toward the end of the ceremony, the groom will give an *arras*, which is a small treasure box filled with fake money to the bride to symbolize that the groom accepts the responsibility of providing for his wife and their future family. And it's just a symbol of that. The reception is held at the groom's family's house and of course there's lots of dancing and music and they also give presents as they do here in the states.

These four customs are customs that both cultures celebrate but celebrate in different ways. They are, you know, the same but different. I hope I have enlightened you, given you some information that you might not have had before. And if you have any questions, please feel free to ask and I'll try to answer.

SPEECH EVALUATION FORM

SPEAKER Stephanie Herrera   **TOPIC** "Same Holidays, Different Customs"   **DATE** _____

Overall Considerations

4	Did the speaker seem committed to the topic?
5	Did the speech meet the requirements of the assignment?
4	Was the speech adapted to fit the audience?
5	Did the speech promote identification among topic, audience, and speaker?
5	Was the purpose of the speech clear?
4	Was the topic handled with imagination and freshness?
5	Did the speech meet high ethical standards?

Substance

5	Was the topic worthwhile?
3	Had the speaker done sufficient research?
4	Were the main ideas supported with reliable and relevant information?
3	Was testimony used appropriately?
4	Were the sources documented appropriately?
5	Were examples or narratives used effectively?
5	Was the reasoning clear and correct?

Structure

3	Did the introduction spark your interest?
5	Did the introduction adequately preview the message?
5	Was the speech easy to follow?
5	Could you identify the main points of the speech?
4	Were transitions used to tie the speech together?
3	Did the conclusion summarize the message?
2	Did the conclusion help you remember the speech?

Presentation

5	Was the language clear, simple, and direct?
5	Was the language colorful?
5	Were grammar and pronunciations correct?
4	Was the speech presented extemporaneously?
3	Were notes used unobtrusively?
5	Was the speaker appropriately enthusiastic?
4	Did the speaker maintain good eye contact?
5	Did gestures and body language complement ideas?
5	Was the speaker's voice expressive?
5	Were the rate and loudness appropriate to the material?
4	Did the speaker uses pauses appropriately?
1	Did presentation aids make the message clearer or more memorable?
1	Were presentation aids skillfully integrated into the speech?
4	Was the presentation free from distracting mannerisms?

Discussion Guide for "Same Holidays, Different Customs"

1. What is the purpose of Stephanie's informative speech?

2. What kind of informative speech does Stephanie develop?

3. What major forms of supporting materials does she use, and what learning principles does she apply?

4. What speech design does Stephanie follow?

5. What are the major strengths and weaknesses of her presentation?

Commentary on "Same Holidays, Different Customs"

Chapter 12 notes that the general function of informative speeches is to share knowledge. Stephanie Herrera takes advantage of her cultural background to share knowledge of rituals that are important in Mexican family life. While her major purpose is to share information, Stephanie's sympathetic portrayal also dignifies the customs of a people who have often been derogated in the folklore and media images of their northern neighbor. To that subtle extent, she may also reform the perceptions of some listeners. It is hard not to conclude, for example, that the Mexican "Day of the Dead" ceremonies, which honor and remember deceased loved ones, are far more serious and respectful than those practised on Halloween in much of the United States.

Stephanie's speech is best described as descriptive. She offers appealing word-pictures of the ceremonies she describes. The major supporting materials she uses are personal testimony and stories told by her mother. The major learning principles she applies are to gain and hold audience attention through colorful descriptions that make her subject come to life and that align with similar customs in the United States. The resulting contrasts make the rituals she describes seem relevant as well as interesting on their own.

The major speech design Stephanie employs is categorical, in that each main point describes an important ceremony in Mexican life. She also uses comparative design in that each ceremony implies a comparison and contrast with a like ceremony familiar to her audience.

The charming, engaging speech Stephanie presents might have been even more effective had she brought as presentation aids objects illustrating the various ceremonies she describes (such as the *lasso*). Her speech opening seems rather ordinary, and her preview promises an order of topics different from what actually occurs. She should also have done additional research to strengthen the knowledge base of her speech. This might have allowed her to present expert testimony to reinforce her mother's account of the social, cultural significance of the ceremonies. She is too dependent on notes at certain points, and at one time slips into what might be described as a freudian malapropism, as she uses "rite of passion" instead of "rite of passage" to describe the coming-out ceremony for fifteen-year-old girls. The conclusion of her speech could have been more imaginative.

On the whole, we think this informative speech communicates effectively on a well-chosen topic but that it missed some opportunities to be better. We would assign a "B" grade.

Differences Between Chinese and American Students

Lily Geng

China is a country totally different from America. It has a long history of more than several thousand years. So, when I first came to U.S.A., there are lots of people that were curious about China. They ask me about China, how it looks like, and something about Chinese people. So here, I want to talk about some main differences between the Chinese college students and American college students.

First, I want to talk [about] the Chinese students and the American students, they have different views of being individualistic. So, in China when we go to the college, normally we will leave our family, go to another city, to some important cities with a lot of universities there. So, when we were elementary or high school students we just stay home. We have to abide by what the parents said. So when we really get our freedom we just change totally different. We have more freedom to go out to enjoy and to do everything on your own. So, once, I can give an example here, one of my friends, at first he was a elementary school student and he was very quiet—he just studied, keep on studying, nothing else. But after he graduated from that school he went to the University and he just changed. He went to dance, and he went outside to hike, go hiking, everything. He just changed a lot. But here—in Chinese University, the students emphasize more being individual, being an individual—but here, when I came here, I found American students after they went to the University they become more uniform. Because the main goal to go to the University is to find a better job here. So the normal American companies they want you to be more professional. I mean you have to dress and you have to talk in a certain way. Such things like that. So they become more, I mean less, individual.

And the second point is in China as a student we have to spend more time on studying. Normally after we took all the classes for the whole day, we have to spend maybe four or five hours during the night to study by yourself. But here, when I came here, . . . American students they will spend more time on going out to work and on parties and when I first came here I found so many parties I was real surprised. And I thought maybe that's the main difference. They hold a different view about studying. In China we have the pressures from finding a better job because we find a better job only if we can get better grades. If we cannot, normally we cannot find a better job. But here, American students, they emphasize more their experience during their undergraduate school. So, they will go out to work and they will support themselves but in China, we just support, gather money from our family so it's totally different too.

And the last point I want to mention is the relationship between the professors and the students. Here the students pay the tuition and they think they should get from the professors. So they will hold the attitude that they paid tuition and the professors are responsible to answer any kind of their questions. But in China we will show more respect to the professors. For example, during the class we won't question the professors, if he has some maybe wrong ideas [in] our opinions. We would just keep quiet and after the class maybe we will ask him individually or personally. We won't embarrass the professors. But here, sometimes when I was in a class, I found there were some students that won't care so much and if they have any question, even something about the professor's personal views, they will ask directly. So, that's another surprise to me.

So, . . . [these contrasts] I mention, I think they are mainly because [of] the culture differences between Chinese students and American students. Maybe as a foreigner, they [Chinese] will feel very shocked or sometimes they will feel strange. But as the time passes they will accept all the views. At least they [will] adjust . . . to the American culture. Okay that's all. Thank you.

SPEECH EVALUATION FORM

SPEAKER Lisa Geng   **TOPIC** "Differences Between Chinese and American Students"   **DATE** _____

Overall Considerations

  4   Did the speaker seem committed to the topic?
  4   Did the speech meet the requirements of the assignment?
  4   Was the speech adapted to fit the audience?
  3   Did the speech promote identification among topic, audience, and speaker?
  4   Was the purpose of the speech clear?
  3   Was the topic handled with imagination and freshness?
  3   Did the speech meet high ethical standards?

Substance

  5   Was the topic worthwhile?
  1   Had the speaker done sufficient research?
  2   Were the main ideas supported with reliable and relevant information?
  2   Was testimony used appropriately?
  1   Were the sources documented appropriately?
  3   Were examples or narratives used effectively?
  2   Was the reasoning clear and correct?

Structure

  3   Did the introduction spark your interest?
  2   Did the introduction adequately preview the message?
  3   Was the speech easy to follow?
  4   Could you identify the main points of the speech?
  2   Were transitions used to tie the speech together?
  2   Did the conclusion summarize the message?
  2   Did the conclusion help you remember the speech?

Presentation

  2   Was the language clear, simple, and direct?
  3   Was the language colorful?
  3   Were grammar and pronunciations correct?
  5   Was the speech presented extemporaneously?
  5   Were notes used unobtrusively?
  4   Was the speaker appropriately enthusiastic?
  5   Did the speaker maintain good eye contact?
  4   Did gestures and body language complement ideas?
  5   Was the speaker's voice expressive?
  4   Were the rate and loudness appropriate to the material?
  3   Did the speaker uses pauses appropriately?
  NA   Did presentation aids make the message clearer or more memorable?
  NA   Were presentation aids skillfully integrated into the speech?
  4   Was the presentation free from distracting mannerisms?

Discussion Guide for "Differences Between Chinese and American Students"

1. What type of informative speech does Lily Geng develop and what kind of design does she use?

2. What are the strengths of Lily's presentation?

3. How might she have improved this speech?

4. What value might this speech have for the critical, constructive listener?

Commentary on "Differences Between Chinese and American Students"

The function of Lily Geng's informative speech is to share information and ideas. Hers is a speech of explanation, dealing with cultural differences between Chinese and American college students. The speech is built upon a combined categorical and comparative design.

Lily is an obviously intelligent student who could well become an impressive speaker. She has a melodic and expressive voice and seems pleasant and likable. The topic is well selected for her audience of American classmates, almost assuring an interested audience. Why then, is this speech not more successful?

Our first answer is that Lily neglected to help her listeners learn. Her introduction should have done more to gain audience attention and to motivate listeners. She needed also to preview her main points, and, while her struggle with spoken English is understandable, she needed to word her points more clearly. Better transitions might have tied the speech together more effectively. Obviously, she failed to develop a conclusion that adequately summarized and reflected upon the meaning of her message. In short, the speech needed more artfully to encourage constructive listening.

The second serious problem with this speech is that it relies too much on casual personal knowledge to support its observations. The speech does not meet the requirements of *responsible knowledge,* discussed in Chapter 5. At times Lily drifts into stereotype, an especially ironical fault, in that she represents a people who themselves have often been victimized by stereotype. At the very least, Lily's generalizations need the support of good research and expert testimony, and she needs more and clearer examples.

For all of these flaws, Lily Geng's speech does offer some interesting claims. It is useful to be able to see ourselves from a perspective outside our own culture. When that perspective reveals that we may encourage too much conformity, that we don't take higher education as seriously as we might, and that we don't respect sufficiently those who have devoted themselves to learning, a little change may be in order. Therefore, Lily's speech may have value for its listeners. We would give it a "C" grade.

Fibrocystic Breast Disease

Markisha Webster

Many of you sitting in this room today, male and female, are well aware of female health problems. You have either learned about them through a health class, through friends, or through your relatives. One disease that everyone has heard about is cancer. And in particular, breast cancer. Well I'm not here today to talk to you about breast cancer. But I am here today to talk to you about a disease that could be related to breast cancer. I, like many young women, did not think about what was going on in my body at the age of sixteen. I knew that my body was changing and preparing me for womanhood, but I didn't think about any specific problems. That was until I was diagnosed with the disease that I am here to talk about, fibrocystic breast disease. I will tell you about what it is and how it can be detected, why it can be an important health issue, and some preventive steps that could help to reduce the chance of getting it.

Well I'm sure some of you are like, "fibro *who*?" The first point I want to make is related to what the disease really is. In this condition of the breast, many small cysts are produced owing to an overgrowth of the fibrous tissue in the area of the ducts. The condition is thought to be caused by hormonal imbalance during the monthly cycle changes with failure of normal reaction to the breast following the monthly cycle activities. The female sex hormones, estrogen and proestrogen, are not balanced properly. The cysts may be singular or multiple and could increase in size or stay the same. And the amazing thing is to believe that they can increase in size within a matter of a few days. They can go from a size of a quarter to the size of your entire breast. The important thing to remember is that they should be noted as lumps. This does not mean that they are malignant but it also does not guarantee that they are not. As mentioned before, they are related to a woman's menstrual cycle, and this is the point at which many women discover them. The cysts are usually soft and tender and movable, if touched or pressed under examining fingers. They normally occur in women between the ages of thirty and menopause. But in my research I found that women of my age group between sixteen and twenty are likely to get the disease also.

So now that you know what the condition is, how can it be diagnosed? Many women are told by a doctor or some like me are able to detect the disease on their own. If for any reason you feel lumps that are easy to touch without a lot of pressure, it may be a clear sign. Some cysts are tender and could be painful if touched, but not all. This is really not a good sign because a lot of women experience tenderness in their breasts or in their monthly cycle. One sure sign to me was the sharp shooting pains that would go through my breast occasionally. The best detection of course is your doctor. He or she will be able to decide the best treatment if you are diagnosed with the disease. The first thing that would normally happen is you would be told to have a mammogram, which is a fairly uncomfortable procedure that gives an x-ray of the breast. After this happens you will be told whether or not you'll have a biopsy, which is the removal of the mass, or an aspiration, which is an attempt to draw fluid off of the mass. In my case I was given both. Normally if fluid cannot be drawn an automatic biopsy will be performed.

Now what can all of this lead to? Well it's sad to say that breast cancer is the leading cause of death in women today. That is really the biggest hazard to women that are diagnosed with the disease. Fibrocystic breast disease carriers are more at risk for cancer than those who do not have the disease. The presence of nodular tissue in the breast makes the early detection of breast cancer hard. There may be so many masses that the one containing the cancer cannot be found.

There is really no sure-fire way to prevent yourself if you get stuck with it but there is a way you can keep an eye on what is going on. In addition to that, there are preventive measures that can be taken. The best way to watch and see what your breasts are doing is to have breast self-examinations or to have one done by your doctor. As preventive measures go, a decrease in caffeine and nicotine should be taken. Also it has been recently found out that women who have had children and are breast-feeding can reduce their chances of further development of cysts. And it can also limit the growth of any masses that can be related to cancer. It is best to keep in-tune with what your body is doing and here [refers to chart] I have a chart of some things that you should avoid: caffeine and this also includes chocolate, any kind of chocolate candy or anything like that. And nicotine, nicotine products, anything with tobacco. On this side [turns the poster over] I have an example of a breast self-examination. And it can be done in the shower, before a mirror, or lying down. And this little piece of paper here is to hang in your shower, it's like a shower hang-tag. Normally lying down is the best way to get a full examination because you are able to check everything.

In conclusion, remember to have regular checkups and never take anything that may seem a little strange as just nothing. Detecting problems early could save your life. In addition to all of that, keep in mind that diseases have no names and as a young adult and woman it is important not to rule yourself out for any health problems. I am a prime example of what can happen to people who just don't take care of themselves like they should. Now I take anything dealing with female health seriously. Thank you.

SPEECH EVALUATION FORM

SPEAKER Markisha Webster   **TOPIC** "Fibrocystic Breast Disease"   **DATE** _____

Overall Considerations

- __5__ Did the speaker seem committed to the topic?
- __5__ Did the speech meet the requirements of the assignment?
- __4__ Was the speech adapted to fit the audience?
- __4__ Did the speech promote identification among topic, audience, and speaker?
- __5__ Was the purpose of the speech clear?
- __3__ Was the topic handled with imagination and freshness?
- __5__ Did the speech meet high ethical standards?

Substance

- __5__ Was the topic worthwhile?
- __5__ Had the speaker done sufficient research?
- __5__ Were the main ideas supported with reliable and relevant information?
- __1__ Was testimony used appropriately?
- __1__ Were the sources documented appropriately?
- __2__ Were examples or narratives used effectively?
- __5__ Was the reasoning clear and correct?

Structure

- __5__ Did the introduction spark your interest?
- __5__ Did the introduction adequately preview the message?
- __5__ Was the speech easy to follow?
- __5__ Could you identify the main points of the speech?
- __4__ Were transitions used to tie the speech together?
- __3__ Did the conclusion summarize the message?
- __3__ Did the conclusion help you remember the speech?

Presentation

- __4__ Was the language clear, simple, and direct?
- __4__ Was the language colorful?
- __5__ Were grammar and pronunciations correct?
- __4__ Was the speech presented extemporaneously?
- __3__ Were notes used unobtrusively?
- __5__ Was the speaker appropriately enthusiastic?
- __4__ Did the speaker maintain good eye contact?
- __4__ Did gestures and body language complement ideas?
- __5__ Was the speaker's voice expressive?
- __5__ Were the rate and loudness appropriate to the material?
- __4__ Did the speaker uses pauses appropriately?
- __2__ Did presentation aids make the message clearer or more memorable?
- __2__ Were presentation aids skillfully integrated into the speech?
- __5__ Was the presentation free from distracting mannerisms?

Discussion Guide for "Fibrocystic Breast Disease"

1. In what special way does Markisha Webster gain attention for her speech?

2. What design does Markisha use for her speech, and what main points does she develop within it?

3. What is her major kind of supporting material? What other kinds might she have used?

4. If you were advising Markisha, what strengths would you praise, and what areas needing improvement would you point out to her?

Commentary on "Fibrocystic Breast Disease"

Markisha Webster's informative speech of explanation gains audience attention in the most compelling of ways: she herself is a victim of the disease she is describing. Markisha demonstrates how to handle a serious, mature topic with taste and discretion. Having established her personal connection with it, she proceeds to discuss it objectively and dispassionately, never embarrassing her listeners, but not letting them forget either her own involvement and commitment.

Markisha develops her speech in a categorical design, developing four main points that include definition, diagnosis, consequences, and prevention. She gains attention very effectively, involves her listeners, and previews her speech nicely. She makes a good transition from definition to diagnosis, but she needed a better transition from consequences to prevention. In the latter stages of the speech, her description becomes almost too clinical, and she runs the risk of losing a few listeners. Her conclusion seems rather routine in comparison to her beginning, and she needs to involve listeners more. For example, instead of ending with "Now I take anything dealing with female health seriously. Thank you," she should drop the "thank you" and substitute an emphatic final "So should you!"

The main supporting material for Markisha's speech is good solid information. At one point she uses comparison nicely, as she notes that lumps can range from about "the size of a quarter to the size of an entire breast." Throughout, one gains the impression that Markisha is offering responsible knowledge, and she refers more than once to the "research" she has done. But nowhere in her speech does she document any of this research, nor does she make use of any expert testimony from it. We think she missed a golden opportunity to make her speech even more authoritative.

The presentation aid she uses seems ineffective compared to the rest of her speech. The information it offered was either obvious without the aid, as when she advised listeners to avoid coffee and nicotine, or obscure, as when she presented the shower hang-tag that no one—not even in the front row—might have read. A better choice of presentation aids might have been a hand-out of vital information, distributed at the end of her speech. This might have included hang-tags for especially interested listeners. Other aspects of the presentation varied in quality. For the most part she maintained good contact with listeners, using her expressive face and voice to good advantage. At times, however, she made too evident use of her notes and lost eye contact.

Despite these various flaws, we found this speech on the whole to be an often effective discussion of a worthwhile topic, and would give it a high "B."

Physical Fitness

Bridget Plyler

We have all seen the media and the hype in recent years about physical fitness. Physical fitness is not just an asset, it is a necessity. The lack of physically fit people in our society leads to higher cases of osteoporosis, obesity, cancer, heart disease, and increased cases of nervous and emotional stress. The problem originated in the twentieth century with the advances of technology. Automation allows a person to work-in, eat-in, order-in, and even shop-in. Technology affects all age groups—children, teens, young adults, adults, and even seniors. The effects of automation will continue to be detrimental to our society unless we change. High blood pressure, strokes, and heart attacks will afflict a greater portion of the population. Cancer will become a greater risk. Obesity and osteoporosis will occur with higher incidence. And incidence of nervous and emotional stress will grow. The solution to the lack of physically fit Americans is for us to get fit through a healthy diet and exercise.

I have outlined the basic components of a healthy diet recommended by dieticians and physicians. You should eat little fat and cholesterol. This means eating less fatty foods; fried and breaded foods; high-fat sweets like cakes, cookies, and chocolate; and less fatty meats. You should eat less sodium. This means less than 2000 milligrams a day. Read the back of your chip packages. Eat more complex carbohydrates. This means eating more bread, pasta, corn, and potatoes. You should also eat more fruit. These are high in fiber and low in cholesterol, fat, and salt. Also you should eat more vegetable protein rather than animal protein. Vegetable protein can be found in dried peas and beans. It's got low fat and cholesterol and great protein. Finally you should avoid saturated fats, which have been linked to heart disease and the rise of cholesterol and blood levels. Saturated fats and cholesterol can be found in foods like steak, butter, and cheese. Vegetable foods don't have cholesterol but some can have fats. Examples are margarine, nuts, and chocolate.

The next important step in a healthy diet involves sticking to it, even when you're eating out. Order broiled, baked, steamed, and poached foods. Don't eat the breaded or fried foods that are high in cholesterol and saturated fat. Order all of your sauces on the side. A good rule of thumb is two teaspoons for every sauce or dressing. And save desserts for special occasions and then share. Finally, remember to ask [the waiter]. It's your health.

Not only do you need a healthy diet for becoming physically fit but you also need to exercise. How you should exercise depends on how fit you are. Out-of-shape people should exercise short amounts of time and rest equal amounts of time. According to Covert Bailey, author of *Getting Fit, Burning Fat, and Exercising Right*, [he] says, "aerobic exercise can be done frequently as long as you remember the rule, aerobic means not out of breath." When exercising, do the long steady part of your exercise at the low end of aerobic capabilities. Add short periods of intense exercise. Intense exercise is a relative term. It means pushing yourself beyond what you can do. Examples would be wind sprints, cross training, or weight lifting. The amount of muscle exercised means the more benefit you get. For example, if you exercise walking for forty minutes it will be equivalent to only cycling for twenty minutes.

The next question is where to exercise? If you want to exercise at home and at a low cost, Doctor Wayne Wescott, Ph. D. and national consultant for the Y.W.C.A., suggests using a program with twenty minutes of strength exercise, twenty minutes of endurance exercise, and a low-fat nutrition plan. For the twenty minutes of endurance exercise all you need is a pair of legs. For the low-fat nutrition plan you need a refrigerator and maybe a wellness book which lists the fat contents of foods. For strength Dr. Wescott suggests using dumbbells, saying dumbbells provide excellent resistance, place minimal stress on wrists, elbows, and pose little injury risks. They also offer unlimited exercise variety and require little training or storage space and have a low price tag. For a detailed description of Dr. Wescott's dumbbell workout, check out the June, 1994 issue of *Prevention*.

If you want to work out at a health club, you can use the University of Memphis facilities or join a private health club. The University of Memphis offers a nautilus room and a weight training room to all students free of charge, Monday through Friday, 3:30 p.m. to 10 p.m. If you want to join a private health club, John McCarthy, executive director for the Association of Quality Clubs, gives a few tips on finding good clubs. He says, "Read the fine print. You may be signing on for an unlimited membership. Don't sign for a membership for longer than one year. You or the club may not stick. And remember, get what you pay for, quality and cleanliness." Local clubs range from about twenty five dollars a month to fifty dollars a month with varying initiation fees. Some local clubs are the Y.M.C.A. located off the south side of campus, there is Gold's Gym located across from the Oak Court mall, we have the Q Sports Club located on Ridgeway, and the French Riviera Spa is located downtown and also in East Memphis.

The person responsible for putting my plan into action is you. I realize that some of you may feel you have good reasons not to be physically fit. You feel you're normally active or busy and don't need to exercise. Some of you may be afraid that if you exercise you will eat more and gain weight. Another reason may be that you sometimes feel the seemingly inevitable pain that comes from exercise. Or you may feel tired at the end of a long day and don't want to exercise. And finally, you may feel you just don't have enough time. I have an answer for each of these objections. If you're normally busy or active you can increase your productivity by twenty percent, just by exercising twenty-five to thirty-five minutes a day. If you exercise in moderation, you won't gain weight, but you'll stabilize your blood sugar levels and make your eating habits easier to control. Fatigue results from a lack of oxygen to the body. Exercise helps increase the amount of oxygen your body can take up and will increase your energy levels. The theory of "no pain, no gain" is ludicrous. The only thing that pain tells you is you're hurting your body. And finally, with an increased productivity of twenty percent and increased energy levels, finding that extra thirty minutes a day to work out should be easy.

The final most important thing is to pick an exercise that you enjoy. Being physically fit provides many advantages. The number of heart attacks, strokes, and high blood pressure cases will decrease. The number of cancer cases will also decrease. Osteoporosis and obesity will occur with lower incidence. And cases of nervous and emotional stress will be lower.

Remember nutrition is important. Eat a low-fat, low-cholesterol, and low-salt diet. And remember to eat lots of fiber, vegetable protein, and complex carbohydrates. The more you exercise, the less time you need to spend exercising. Exercising can be inexpensive and even free. The University of Memphis has facilities available free of charge to all students in the athletic building from 3:30 pm. to 10 p.m. Monday through Friday. You can work out at home for free or you can join a local gym that fits your needs and budgets. It's time to get up, get out, and get fit.

SPEECH EVALUATION FORM

SPEAKER Bridget Plyler _____ **TOPIC** "Physical Fitness" _____ **DATE** _____

Overall Considerations

4	Did the speaker seem committed to the topic?
3	Did the speech meet the requirements of the assignment?
3	Was the speech adapted to fit the audience?
2	Did the speech promote identification among topic, audience, and speaker?
3	Was the purpose of the speech clear?
2	Was the topic handled with imagination and freshness?
5	Did the speech meet high ethical standards?

Substance

5	Was the topic worthwhile?
5	Had the speaker done sufficient research?
4	Were the main ideas supported with reliable and relevant information?
4	Was testimony used appropriately?
4	Were the sources documented appropriately?
1	Were examples or narratives used effectively?
3	Was the reasoning clear and correct?

Structure

2	Did the introduction spark your interest?
3	Did the introduction adequately preview the message?
3	Was the speech easy to follow?
3	Could you identify the main points of the speech?
3	Were transitions used to tie the speech together?
2	Did the conclusion summarize the message?
2	Did the conclusion help you remember the speech?

Presentation

3	Was the language clear, simple, and direct?
2	Was the language colorful?
5	Were grammar and pronunciations correct?
2	Was the speech presented extemporaneously?
2	Were notes used unobtrusively?
2	Was the speaker appropriately enthusiastic?
3	Did the speaker maintain good eye contact?
2	Did gestures and body language complement ideas?
1	Was the speaker's voice expressive?
3	Were the rate and loudness appropriate to the material?
1	Did the speaker uses pauses appropriately?
1	Did presentation aids make the message clearer or more memorable?
NA	Were presentation aids skillfully integrated into the speech?
3	Was the presentation free from distracting mannerisms?

Discussion Guide for "Physical Fitness"

1. Does Bridget sufficiently narrow her topic?

2. Evaluate Bridget's use of supporting material.

3. How might Bridget have increased her sense of audience contact?

Commentary on "Physical Fitness"

Bridget Plyler offers a largely informative speech of explanation that develops within a categorical design. Bridget began with the admirable goal of awakening her listeners to the need for better physical fitness. While she did a good deal of research for her speech, ultimately her effort was compromised by two large problems: (1) she tried to accomplish too much, and (2) she was not sufficiently sensitive to her listeners' needs.

The first problem, common to beginning students, comes when they want so much to accomplish large, lofty goals that they forget to focus on a topic they can discuss adequately within time limits. Developing within Bridget's categorical design are two main points: (1) listeners should follow a healthy diet, and (2) listeners should develop an effective exercise program. As it turns out, either of these points could have constituted a speech in itself. Crowded as they are into one speech, neither is sufficiently developed. The main point on nutrition, for example, suffers from a lack of supporting materials. Bridget describes accurately the essentials of good nutrition, but she does not document her points or develop good expert testimony. Nor does she make her ideas come to life through good specific examples or stories or through an effective presentation aid. Her language, as well, is somewhat lifeless. Her main point on exercise is more fully documented and demonstrates the range of her preparation. But again, she needed to bring her ideas to life through effective examples and stories.

She extends the range of her topic even further as she considers local exercise gyms, evaluates their offerings, and cautions about entering long-term contractual obligations with them. While this subject might also constitute a speech in itself, Bridget does adapt at this point to her listeners' possible interest in starting an exercise program. As her speech winds down, Bridget launches into what at first seems a persuasive tag-on to her speech, countering possible audience objections to the pain and trouble of undertaking an effective overall program of physical fitness. This tag-on to her speech strains an already hyperextended topic and raises the question of whether her general function is to inform or persuade. Actually, she might have worked this material somewhat differently into the beginning of her speech to motivate listeners and to engage their attention. Then she could have proceeded to develop one of her main points effectively as a single complete speech. She might also have considered a question-answer format in which she would have anticipated possible audience questions, then answered them. That approach might have engaged listeners more fully in her speech. She could then have pursued her other main point in a subsequent speech.

This insensitivity to the need for motivating material is symptomatic of a deeper problem. Bridget develops little sense of communicative contact with her listeners. Too often her face is not expressive, and her voice lacks variety and interest. She reads her notes too much, and speaks in a rapid, staccato rate that hurries her listeners without giving them time to contemplate her meaning. She needs very much to develop the art of the pause.

These problems severely harmed some worthy research work on her part and prevented her speech from having much impact on listeners. We would have assigned a "C" grade.

Common Herbs

Lee Harden

Have you heard people talking about using things like sassafras and ginger roots to cure common ailments and probably thought it was kind of silly and old fashioned? I used to think like that too. Until I was around the age of ten. That's when I spent the weekend over at my grandmother's house. I had this terrible toothache. Okay, well she gave me one of two options. One, you can take one piece of a string and tie it to your tooth and take the other end and tie it to a doorknob. Slam it shut! Or two, you can go into my cabinet and taste one of my herbal mixtures. So of course, I chose to go into the cabinet and get the herbal mixture. Okay, to my surprise, the next day my toothache was gone. Ever since then I have been paying attention when my grandmother would talk to me about her herbal medicines and remedies. I've also been reading guides and references to learn more about them. So today I would like to share with you all what I have learned so that you can know how common herbs such as coriander, white willow bark, and celery seeds can be used as an alternative route as to waiting long hours in the doctors' offices and spending so much money on high expensive prescriptions which may do exactly the same things.

But first, we must talk about how herbs are commonly prepared. You see, before any herb can actually be used for its therapeutic or healing powers it must usually be dried first. This can be done by either hanging it in bunches in a cool dry place or placing it in the oven on a cookie sheet at 350 degrees Fahrenheit for about twenty minutes. Or you can buy a common produce dryer. Now once the herbs have been dried they can be made into four different preparations which I have listed here [refers to presentation aid]: powders, tinctures, decoctions, and infusions.

Now powders are generally made by taking the herb and grinding them with a mortar and pestle or nowadays you can buy a basic grinder, like a coffee grinder or a produce grinder, to suffice. Now tinctures is a very interesting thing. You take one ounce of the herb and you mix it with five ounces of grain alcohol. Now grain alcohol is one hundred and ninety eight percent pure. So regardless, you won't feel the effects because you will probably be drunk. Okay, for those of you all who don't drink alcohol you can substitute apple cider vinegar. Since it is very strong, it is commonly known for it to be stored for like six weeks.

Decoctions is fairly common. You take one ounce of the bark or root of the particular herb and you boil it or steep it in one ounce of water for about five to twenty minutes. Okay, infusions, which is the most common way the herbs are prepared, is similar to like tea, you take one ounce of the leaves or seeds and you steep it or boil it in the water for five to twenty minutes, one ounce of water.

Okay, in fact the toothache remedy that I mentioned earlier that my grandma made me take, or suggested that I take, was a mixture of the next herb I am going to talk about, coriander. Okay, coriander is not also just good for doing toothaches. It is also known for its ability to relieve pain or indigestion and stomach problems. It's been known since ancient times. In fact it's mentioned in the Bible as it says, the Hebrews took manna from heaven and the manna tasted like coriander.

Okay, now since we're talking about things related to stomach pains, I'm sure everyone knows someone who doesn't like to take aspirin because of the effects it has on the stomach. You might want to suggest to that person that they take the second herb we are going to discuss, white willow bark. The decoction of white willow bark will not only solve the headache problem but it will have no side effects of stomach pain whatsoever. It has been used by the Chinese since 500 B.C.

Okay, now this third herb that we're going to talk about, I'm sure some of us or probably all of us have eaten at some time or another. We've all eaten a celery stalk but none of us has actually thought that the potency of this small celery seed which produces that stalk is so strong that it was used in ancient times to induce menstruation. And in fact it is shown to cause abortion in lab animals. Also studies have revealed—like statistics have been reported in *The Healing Herb*—that it has an effect that somehow or another lowers blood sugar. So the Drug Administration is studying it for possible use as a diabetic treatment. It has also been shown that it has factors which aid it in stalling or reducing factors from congestive heart failure.

Okay, now these are just a few of the herbs found all around the world to cure anything from acne to cancer. Okay, if you would be interested in finding out more or going to a place to get these, you can go to your local herb shop, like the Squash Blossom Market, which is very popular, it's located on Union and McLain. Or you may go to Maggie's Farm over on Overton Square.

Okay, and also I want you to keep in mind, the next time you hear someone talking about "Well I think I'll get some sassafras root," I don't think you should just overlook that as old fashioned, because you never know. That could be the same thing you're paying a hundred dollars for at your local pharmacy. Okay, so thank you very much.

SPEECH EVALUATION FORM

SPEAKER Lee Harden   **TOPIC** "Common Herbs"   **DATE** _____

Overall Considerations

____4____ Did the speaker seem committed to the topic?
____5____ Did the speech meet the requirements of the assignment?
____4____ Was the speech adapted to fit the audience?
____5____ Did the speech promote identification among topic, audience, and speaker?
____4____ Was the purpose of the speech clear?
____5____ Was the topic handled with imagination and freshness?
____4____ Did the speech meet high ethical standards?

Substance

____4____ Was the topic worthwhile?
____3____ Had the speaker done sufficient research?
____3____ Were the main ideas supported with reliable and relevant information?
____1____ Was testimony used appropriately?
____1____ Were the sources documented appropriately?
____5____ Were examples or narratives used effectively?
____2____ Was the reasoning clear and correct?

Structure

____5____ Did the introduction spark your interest?
____2____ Did the introduction adequately preview the message?
____2____ Was the speech easy to follow?
____2____ Could you identify the main points of the speech?
____1____ Were transitions used to tie the speech together?
____1____ Did the conclusion summarize the message?
____2____ Did the conclusion help you remember the speech?

Presentation

____5____ Was the language clear, simple, and direct?
____5____ Was the language colorful?
____2____ Were grammar and pronunciations correct?
____5____ Was the speech presented extemporaneously?
____5____ Were notes used unobtrusively?
____4____ Was the speaker appropriately enthusiastic?
____5____ Did the speaker maintain good eye contact?
____5____ Did gestures and body language complement ideas?
____5____ Was the speaker's voice expressive?
____5____ Were the rate and loudness appropriate to the material?
____4____ Did the speaker uses pauses appropriately?
____2____ Did presentation aids make the message clearer or more memorable?
____2____ Were presentation aids skillfully integrated into the speech?
____3____ Was the presentation free from distracting mannerisms?

Discussion Guide for "Common Herbs"

1. What are the strengths of this informative speech?

2. Evaluate the structure of Lee's speech.

3. How effectively does Lee document his claims?

4. Evaluate the presentation aid used in this speech.

Commentary on "Common Herbs"

Lee Harden's informative speech of explanation follows what appears to be a categorical design and engages audience interest with a fresh topic, an effective introduction, and an often charming manner of presentation.

Lee does a number of things quite well. His opening makes use of the rhetorical question and narrative, and introduces us to a character we wish he had told us more about, his grandmother. Throughout, Lee uses gesture, facial expression, and an expressive voice to reinforce his message. He establishes a relaxed, friendly relationship with listeners, occasionally using humor to brighten his presentation. He also appears knowledgeable on his subject.

Unfortunately, this speech also presents a number of problems. A major difficulty is that it does not have a well-developed structure. After the effective opening and an adequate presentation of the thesis statement, Lee's speech begins to wander. It does wander in a fairly coherent direction, as he describes how to prepare herbal medicines, their various forms and varieties, and how to acquire them, but the form remains largely embryonic and even open to question. The overall flow of reasoning might have been clearer had Lee begun by identifying the major forms of herbs and what they might do for listeners, then how one might acquire them, and finally how to prepare them, in other words, an almost exact reversal of what he does. Lee does not preview his speech, and his main points themselves do not come clearly into focus. They are not tied together by transitions; "Okay," the usual signal that he is moving to another point, does not offer the listener much guidance, and becomes instead a kind of distraction. The ending of the speech is quite abrupt—it offers no summary and little reflection upon the meaning of Lee's message.

The substance of Lee's speech also was defective. While he seems to know what he's talking about, and assures us that he has done much "reading" on his subject, precise evidence of this research rarely surfaces in the speech. We are left largely to take his word for what he says. Many critical listeners might wonder whether such folk medicine is legitimate, and in fact whether it might be even dangerous, should one rely upon it over more traditional medical care. Thorough documentation of the claims made and establishing the credentials of one's authorities would seem necessary to validate the speech.

Finally, Lee needed to consider other strategies for developing his presentation aid. The single chart he uses is much too busy to convey all the meaning he would like it to, and the writing is too small to be read easily from even the middle row of a normal classroom audience. A series of sequence charts presented on a flip chart would have been a better strategy. Finally, he should have used bold, bright colors rather than pastels to make his aids readable and his points emphatic.

Balancing these various strengths and weaknesses, we would have assigned a "C+" grade. Since the problems of the speech are technical and easily remedied, we would challenge Lee to correct them for his next presentation.

PERSUASIVE SPEECHES

Trade Policies and Human Rights Abuses in China

Lisa Stanley

Can you remember where you were June 4th, 1989? For most of us it was probably the beginning of summer, free and lazy days, maybe a summer job, but most of all it meant freedom. On the other side of the world things were a little bit different. Students in China were fighting for basic rights and reforms in their government, for basic human rights denied them by their government. In the Tiananmen Square incident in 1989, some three thousand student protestors and citizens were killed. Many of these protestors remain in jail today. Although this may not be a really hot topic when compared with other topics, I feel that it is important because we are all students and we enjoy the rights in a democratic society here in the U.S. The question I raise today is, should the U.S. continue a privileged trade status with a country that has such a horrible record of human rights?

First, we should consider what this trade status is. MFN means Most Favored Nations status. President Carter extended this privilege to China, and in 1990, 1991, and '92 this status was brought up again by Congress and tried to be removed. It was because of the Tiananmen Square incident and several other human rights abuses that had occurred in China. All such efforts were vetoed by the president. Basically what this means is that China can export goods into our country with very low tariffs. This decreases their costs of exports and increases their profits. But what kind of human rights abuses are we really talking about?

Keep in mind that China is one of the largest communist governments left in the world today. One example is that the media is highly controlled. Foreign broadcasts such as the "BBC" and "Voice of America" are regularly interrupted and jammed. The government bans all public demonstrations. One important human rights policy is their one-child policy and this requires that every married couple can only have one child. Because of the importance of having a male heir in the Chinese culture, many abortions occur. Chinese press reports show that 97.5 percent of all fetuses aborted are girls. This results in over five hundred thousand more male births than female. These reports may not even be accurate, considering that many people don't report the birth of a girl. Many young girl babies wash up on the shores of beaches and several are sent to orphanages to grow up secretly. More importantly on the political scale is the treatment of political prisoners. People are jailed for even voicing their democratic ideals. Human rights organizations have no visitation policies to these prisons and the International Red Cross has not even been allowed access to China's prisons.

But China defends themselves. They say their culture is based on the Confucian Ethic. This means that some people have a very high social status and some people have a very low. Because of this, they say China's leaders do not have to adhere to the international laws of human rights. If they did this, they say that it would only threaten social stability.

So why does the U.S. put up with it? Why do we continue to offer privileges to a country with such a horrible human rights record? The first answer that comes to many peoples' minds is clear—money. Economic decisions come before moral decisions in the business sector. The advocates of this say that if we continue privileged trade with China we will create an intellectual middle class and this middle class group of people will help promote democratic ideals. How can they do this when people are jailed for just voicing their opinions about what they believe in a democratic society? Plus there is evidence to suggest that this won't work. Almost every spring for the past five years, Congress brings up this trading status for review. And in 1993 because of a campaign promise, President Clinton said he would continue this trade status on a condition, if and only if China made, quote, "overall significant progress in the area of human rights." First of all this is a very vague requirement, overall significant progress. Secondly, journalist Robert Jenning Wright said Asia Watch, an affiliate of Human Rights Watch, published a six hundred and thirty-two page report about the abuses in China and Tibet. This report found that 1993, the year of the campaign promise, was the worst year for human rights abuses compared since 1989 and that is when the Tiananmen Square incident occurred.

Another example against the idea that economics can promote democracy comes from political prisoner Harry Wu. He was an activist in China for many years and served nineteen years in China's prisons. He recently was released, immigrated to the U.S., and became a citizen. Harry was again arrested this year because of trying to enter China. He was soon released under U.S. pressure, but while he was there he noticed that several of the prison guards were using Motorola telephones. Although he realizes this company is making a good business in China, he also sees the phones as another media to help promote the spread of communism and the repressiveness of the Chinese government.

In spring of last year, 1994, the status was brought up again. This time Clinton had an answer. He said that instead of pressing China to reform he completely disassociated human rights abuses with trade rights. He said that a country's human rights record had nothing to do with their trading status. The U.S. chose to make their stance verbal, they chose a passive stance. In June of the same year, China passed a whole new set of regulations against the freedom of association, religion, and assembly.

I understand the position that the U.S. is taking and I also understand that China provides an enormous political and economic link to Asia. But I think that this will be an important issue in the long run. Many people are not even interested. Who cares what goes on in China? Basically what we see is that China is playing trade relations like a toy. We offer them this trade status at very low cost only if they would improve. They didn't improve and we gave them the status anyway. I agree that business and economics is important but I also agree that the U.S. has a very strong position in the international arena. If we could toughen our stance with China, I feel that this could help democratize the country instead of promoting economics and business as far as democratic ideals. In the long run we could help eliminate the communist government and have a better partner for the future.

SPEECH EVALUATION FORM

SPEAKER Lisa Stanley   **TOPIC** "Trade Policies and Human Rights Abuses in China"   **DATE** _____

Overall Considerations

5	Did the speaker seem committed to the topic?
4	Did the speech meet the requirements of the assignment?
5	Was the speech adapted to fit the audience?
4	Did the speech promote identification among topic, audience, and speaker?
4	Was the purpose of the speech clear?
4	Was the topic handled with imagination and freshness?
5	Did the speech meet high ethical standards?

Substance

5	Was the topic worthwhile?
4	Had the speaker done sufficient research?
3	Were the main ideas supported with reliable and relevant information?
3	Was testimony used appropriately?
4	Were the sources documented appropriately?
4	Were examples or narratives used effectively?
5	Was the reasoning clear and correct?

Structure

4	Did the introduction spark your interest?
2	Did the introduction adequately preview the message?
3	Was the speech easy to follow?
3	Could you identify the main points of the speech?
3	Were transitions used to tie the speech together?
3	Did the conclusion summarize the message?
3	Did the conclusion help you remember the speech?

Presentation

5	Was the language clear, simple, and direct?
5	Was the language colorful?
5	Were grammar and pronunciations correct?
3	Was the speech presented extemporaneously?
3	Were notes used unobtrusively?
4	Was the speaker appropriately enthusiastic?
4	Did the speaker maintain good eye contact?
3	Did gestures and body language complement ideas?
5	Was the speaker's voice expressive?
5	Were the rate and loudness appropriate to the material?
3	Did the speaker uses pauses appropriately?
NA	Did presentation aids make the message clearer or more memorable?
NA	Were presentation aids skillfully integrated into the speech?
5	Was the presentation free from distracting mannerisms?

Discussion Guide for "Trade Policies and Human Rights Abuses in China"

1. In terms of the persuasive process discussed in Chapter 13, what are Lisa Stanley's major challenges in this speech?

2. What is the design of her speech, and how would you assess its structural strengths and weaknesses?

3. How adequate is the substance of this speech? Does she use sufficient supporting materials? Does Lisa document and support her major assertions? Does she satisfy the critical listener in you?

4. Evaluate Lisa's use of language and the strengths and weaknesses of her presentation.

Commentary on "Trade Policies and Human Rights Abuses in China"

Lisa Stanley told us that she selected her topic because it was important to her, even though she knew that others in her class might not share her keen interest. In terms of the persuasive process discussed in Chapter 13, she faced the primary tasks of raising awareness, increasing understanding, and securing agreement with her recommendations. As a persuader, she might also have encouraged listeners to enact her recommendations and to integrate them into their belief systems. Her first task, however, was to convince listeners that they had something at stake in the issue she discussed. This is why she begins her speech by asking listeners where they were on June 4, 1989, and why she puts so much stress on *freedom*. By connecting her listeners with that fateful day and by emphasizing a value they shared with Chinese students, she hoped to build identification with victims of the Tiananmen Square outrage and against their oppressors.

Lisa's speech addresses attitudes and values. In terms of its structure, her speech is interesting for a number of reasons. After her effective opening, she offers her thesis statement in the form of a rhetorical question: "Should we continue to offer a privileged trade status to a country with such a horrible record of human rights?" Thereafter, her speech develops two main points in an overall categorical design. First, she must prove that China does indeed possess such a record of rights abuses. Second, she must disprove those who would award China privileged trading status (MFN) despite their record or in hopes of improving it. However, Lisa neglects to provide a clear preview at the outset to help guide listeners, an especially glaring omission in such a complex speech. She does move right away to define the technical term, "most favored nation." Her definition, however, seems slanted and largely ignores the rationale for MFN. Moreover, she really did need to strengthen her definition with documented expert testimony. Finally, she might have delayed her definition until she was ready to develop her second main point, the wisdom and morality of such status for China.

As she develops her first main point, an indictment of China's human rights record, Lisa continues the categorical design, exploring three major categories of abuse. As she develops the second main point, her critique of the policy of awarding MFN to China despite its rights record, Lisa develops a refutative design. This design within a design creates a rather complex pattern, and develops in a rather muddled way. Her statement of the sub-points within this point needed to be sharper and clearer. She also needed a transition and an internal summary between the two main points to keep the listener on track.

As she concluded her speech, Lisa needed clearer recommendations. Suggesting that we "toughen our stance" is probably too vague to be useful. Also, she needed to tell her listeners what *they* could do to encourage such a stance. Finally, she needed a better, more memorable conclusion.

Lisa was justifiably proud of the library work she had done for her speech. She told us: "I felt confident in the research I had done and the position I was presenting." Yet Lisa fails to satisfy critical listeners that her knowledge is responsible and complete. She does not cite one source while building her case against the Chinese human rights record in her first main point. While she draws up a specific indictment, we have to take her word for the assertions she offers. While she documents her second main point more carefully, she fails to support the key assertion that "economic decisions come before moral decisions in business," and she fails to cite the basis for her unflattering paraphrase of President Clinton's position. We think that she did not reveal the substantive basis of her speech to best advantage.

In terms of presentation and style, Lisa confessed to us that she felt quite shaky presnting this speech: "I was very insecure about presenting my opinions in a roomful of my peers." Perhaps, but we find many virtues in her presentation. She comes across as a highly intelligent person of equally high character. While she has not yet developed a good extemporaneous style, she certainly has the makings of one: we are especially impressed by her attractive, expressive voice. She does need to learn the value of pausing to emphasize and introduce points she has just made and will make. And of course she needs to rehearse so that she is less dependent on notes.

Lisa's sense of colorful and powerful language is impressive. Her image of infant girls in China "washing up on the shores of beaches" is quite vivid. She knows how to use the power language we discuss in Chapter 10, culturetypes such as *freedom, human rights, abortion,* and *communism.* She associates these emotional symbols with her points in effective ways.

Balancing the pros and cons of this speech, we would award it a "B+" grade.

Top 10 Reasons to Race for the Cure

Mindy Fischer

I would like to share Jill Ireland's opening words from her book, *Life Wish:* "When I was told I had cancer, I would've loved to have talked to someone who had had the disease. I had watched several people close to me suffer from cancer. But unhappily, none of them had survived. It helped me through my initial terror that Happy Rockefeller and Betty Ford had overcome breast cancer. They were walking around, now smiling and healthy, weren't they? I clung to this: if they could do it, so could I."

Race for the Cure is an opportunity for breast cancer survivors to reach out and support others. It is an opportunity for the public to learn about early detection and a chance for everyone to celebrate life. In the book *Breast Cancer*, William McGuire states that the assumption that women will do anything to detect an early symptom is based on two premises that are not necessarily true. The first is that all women fear the loss of their lives more than the loss of their breast. The second is women believe early diagnosis and treatment can eradicate the disease from their bodies with absolute certainty. Race for the Cure is an important way for the public to show their support for breast cancer survivors and early detection. Doctor Phillip Strax states in his book, *Early Detection,* that ninety percent of breast cancer is detected by the woman herself. Early detection helps . . . cure . . . breast cancer. The sooner they find it, the sooner something can be done about it.

One way that you can help is by participating in Race for the Cure. I'd like to present to you the top ten reasons why you should "race for the cure." The first one is you have the opportunity that you could be on television, because the local media will be there and you can see your face on the evening news. Number nine is, you're prepared to shop early, because the race is being held at the shops of Saddle Creek. So you can go and get your exercise and get all warmed up to go hit the stores. Number eight, you can run in honor or in memory of someone that you know that has had breast cancer. Number seven, you get a race packet and this packet is full of exciting things like coupons from sponsors and all sorts of information about early detection and what you can do to help prevent breast cancer.

Number six, this is an opportunity for you to help breast cancer survivors cope with this disease. In *Breast Cancer*, Karin Gyllenskold writes: "In connection with serious illness and stressful medical treatment, patients need to work through their experiences psychologically before, during and after the treatment." Race for the Cure is a wonderful support for before, during, and after the treatment of breast cancer.

Number five, you have the opportunity to meet many local personalities. Ron Olson will be there as one of the hosts along with Karen Paren and some of the other D.J.'s from FM 100. Number four, for those of you who aren't married, you have the possibility to meet dates because the 5K is a race for women only. So all you guys, there are a lot of women out there. And for all you girls, there is a group called Komen for the Cure and it is an all-male support group that helps set up the race. So there is a lot of opportunity to meet people.

Number three, you get to eat great food and win door prizes. We'll be giving away a pair of airline tickets on American Airlines and we'll also be giving a thousand dollar shopping spree to Saddle Creek. Number two, you get a T-shirt to show that you support Race for the Cure and it's beautiful and everybody'll be so envious that you have this great T-shirt. The number one reason to support Race for the Cure, it's a wonderful opportunity to celebrate life. The life that you have and the life that these breast cancer [survivors] are living after breast cancer.

The sun is beginning to show through the dark clouds and a brighter tomorrow is beginning to dawn. You can help it shine brighter by participating in Race for the Cure on October 7th at 8 o'clock at the shops of Saddle Creek.

SPEECH EVALUATION FORM

SPEAKER Mindy Fischer   **TOPIC** "Top 10 Reasons to Race for the Cure"   **DATE** _____

Overall Considerations

5	Did the speaker seem committed to the topic?
5	Did the speech meet the requirements of the assignment?
4	Was the speech adapted to fit the audience?
4	Did the speech promote identification among topic, audience, and speaker?
2	Was the purpose of the speech clear?
5	Was the topic handled with imagination and freshness?
5	Did the speech meet high ethical standards?

Substance

5	Was the topic worthwhile?
5	Had the speaker done sufficient research?
5	Were the main ideas supported with reliable and relevant information?
5	Was testimony used appropriately?
5	Were the sources documented appropriately?
3	Were examples or narratives used effectively?
3	Was the reasoning clear and correct?

Structure

5	Did the introduction spark your interest?
3	Did the introduction adequately preview the message?
4	Was the speech easy to follow?
4	Could you identify the main points of the speech?
3	Were transitions used to tie the speech together?
3	Did the conclusion summarize the message?
3	Did the conclusion help you remember the speech?

Presentation

5	Was the language clear, simple, and direct?
5	Was the language colorful?
5	Were grammar and pronunciations correct?
4	Was the speech presented extemporaneously?
3	Were notes used unobtrusively?
5	Was the speaker appropriately enthusiastic?
4	Did the speaker maintain good eye contact?
4	Did gestures and body language complement ideas?
4	Was the speaker's voice expressive?
5	Were the rate and loudness appropriate to the material?
3	Did the speaker uses pauses appropriately?
5+	Did presentation aids make the message clearer or more memorable?
5	Were presentation aids skillfully integrated into the speech?
5	Was the presentation free from distracting mannerisms?

Discussion Guide for "Top 10 Reasons to Race for the Cure"

1. What is the challenge Mindy confronted in this persuasive speech?

2. Does she develop clear recommendations for her listeners to enact?

3. How effective is her presentation aid? Does it help build a powerful motivation for her listeners to act?

4. How well does the concluding metaphor reinforce Mindy's message?

Commentary on "Top 10 Reasons to Race for the Cure"

In terms of the persuasive process discussed in Chapter 13, Mindy Fischer wished to go beyond raising awareness, achieving understanding, and securing agreement. She wanted her listeners to enact her recommendations. Therefore, her major challenges were, first, to present clear recommendations, and second, to motivate her listeners. As she developed and presented her speech, Mindy met these challenges with varying degrees of success.

She gets off to a fine start by reading a striking quotation from a book by Jill Ireland. Not only does she set a serious, dignified tone for her speech, but she also begins to demonstrate the fine research she has done. Actually, Mindy could have strengthened and developed this beginning even more. She told us she had a very personal motive as she spoke: her grandmother had died of breast cancer before she was born, and this speech honored her memory. Moreover, she had served on the Memphis area "Race for the Cure" Board of Directors. Tasteful references to these facts as a followup to the Ireland quotation might have both moved her listeners and established her ethos firmly as a spokesperson for this cause.

The major problem at the outset of her speech is its rather vague statement of purpose: she wants her listeners to "participate" in the Race for the Cure event. But how long is the run? Can both men and women run? Must the runners be breast cancer survivors? Since her invitation at the start is made to all her listeners, our initial impression is that anyone can run. Later in her speech, we are told that this is a 5K race and that it is for women only. How then, should the men in her audience "participate" in the event? These initial confusions over the precise nature of her recommendations compromise her persuasive effort.

As she presents her rationale for participation, Mindy uses an ingenious technique. She borrows the David Letterman, "top ten reasons" routine and adapts it into a highly original presentation aid. Notice how the "top ten reasons," before she strips off their velcro covers to reveal the reasons underneath, form a composite pink crossed-ribbons design, adapted from the AIDS awareness logo, that signifies breast cancer awareness. As she presents these reasons, there seems to be no particular order among them. They vary in seriousness from getting a free T-shirt to celebrating life. She might have mentioned the lighter, brighter reasons first, building in seriousness so that she concludes with such reasons as honoring the memory of a loved one, helping breast cancer survivors cope, and celebrating life.

Mindy's conclusion is based upon an archetypal metaphor of light and darkness, of the kind we discuss in Chapter 10. While this image is vivid, she needed perhaps a better transition into her conclusion and a better summary before introducing the metaphor. Because it is presented abruptly, it has a contrived quality. Mindy might have prepared for it more effectively by talking about the darkness of breast cancer at the beginning of her speech, preparing listeners for a metaphorical emphasis on the light of breast cancer awareness at the end of her speech.

Factoring these problems in with the superb presentation aid and the fine research effort Mindy exemplifies, we would give this speech a "B+."

Child Sex Slavery in Thailand

Chris Jowers

My previous speech I told you about my work with mediation with youth offenders, how a child can make some stupid choices early on in life but lose the rest of their innocence forever. But there are children in this world who do not have that gift of choice. Andrew Vox, a child defender and noted author, stated that the ultimate evil is when you take away a child's innocence, their dreams and ultimately their life, effectively destroying the rest of the existence that they could ever have. This ultimate evil is real and is going on right now. In Thailand children are being kidnapped and forced into child sex slavery. Their lives are being forever destroyed. But you, a student at the University of Memphis, can make a difference.

Today I'm going to inform you more about child sex slavery, persuade you why you should get involved, and tell you how you can make a difference while you're completely a thousand miles away. The hard facts in the past are that this type of business as you would call it has been going on in Thailand for quite some time and it wasn't until 1991 that any pressure was brought up against it. When an organization called End Child Prostitution in Asian Tourism was founded and they brought pressure up against Prime Minister Chuan, who stated that yes, this type of business is going on in his country. Although people frown upon it, it makes so much money that officials sometimes persuade and actually encourage it. That's the truth, the money is the thing that is making this tourism so horrible.

And here is the harsh reality for the children. Children from newborns to thirteen years of age are being taken away from their homes, sold by their parents and sometimes conned away from their villages. They are taken to major cities throughout Thailand, like Bangkok, put in brothels, sometimes an iron manacle is chained to their ankle and they are chained—sometimes the chain is even welded—to a cot in a diseased room. From then on their lives will be filled with sexual exploitation. The numbers are even worse. In 1994 over two hundred thousand children were reported forced into this slavery and that's a conservative estimate. They say it's probably about a third of the actual number that's going on. Even worse that it is making one-point-five billion dollars in funds for Thailand. With that kind of money it's easy to see why people don't want to do anything about it. Now there are people in Thailand like in the End Child Prostitution in Asian Tourism that are making a difference but the government—it's hands are tied.

With this kind of atrocity going on I really want to persuade you to take action so I'd like to give you some reasons why you should. Number one, apathy is what this business has been thriving on for thirty-some odd years. People in their own country are turning their backs against the voices. Not everyone but some are, and they expect the same thing to happen in the international scene because it has been going on for so long. So if you turn your backs on it you may not be supporting it but you are in a way letting it go on. Also, in this country we have a tremendous gift. We can make a difference in our own society and we have the ability to make a difference in other peoples' society. Groups like Amnesty International have been able to get political prisoners out of foreign countries simply by letter writing campaigns to the government. With that type of action this problem can be changed just by letter writing. Another horrible thing that this sex slavery has brought upon Thailand is the HIV and AIDS virus. Right now over five hundred thousand people have contracted the HIV or AIDS viruses. The numbers are going to climb because Thailand, [where] this atrocity is happening, if it's not stopped in the year 2000, two-point-two-five million people in that one country alone will have contracted the disease. And this is a disease that is on everyone's mind and is going to become everyone's problem. Also the kidnapings are going international. Not only children in Thailand are being stopped. That in itself should be enough but children from China, Laos, and Burma are being taken. Who knows, America may be next on their agenda. The main reason why you should get involved is this can only change by someone taking action. If more and more people take action against it, the problem will begin to decrease and hopefully one day go away.

Now how you can make a difference is easier than you might think. Number one, you can boycott products made in Thailand. The governments are in trade with one another, Thailand and the United States. And if you boycott products made in Thailand you are sending a message first of all to the business. You're saying, look I don't care if you have a factory there, I don't care if this is a great product, this is what is going on in that country and by you having a factory there you are sort of supporting it. And when you do that the companies can then put pressure on the government itself and say, hey, we're not going to put any more factories in here until you change this problem. We would not put factories in a country where racism was openly enforced and charged into but in a country where children are being prostituted nothing is being done about it. Also you can watch these agencies here [refers to chart]. These are the agencies that have been the institutional and have been the primary changing force against child sex slavery in Thailand. The first organization as I have already mentioned is called "End Child Prostitution in Asian Tourism" or ECPAT. Now these are the ones that brought the pressure against Prime Minister Chuan in Thailand itself. Their main base now is in Thailand. Human Rights Watch has been an organization that is trying to change things from an American standpoint. One of the directors, Dorothy Thomas, went to the Senate and cited that in Section 502 of the U.S. Trade Act that the United States Trade Representative to whatever country would have the ability to review their rights. Well, the U.S. Trade Representative that went to Thailand said this was discrimination and not slavery. You can also—with Human Rights Watch— write your senator and your congressman to get them aware of this problem. And finally there is an organization called "Don't Buy Thai." This is the central force of the boycott against Thai products. It's trying to get the message to the American companies and the international companies to quit supporting this by putting major factories there. You can change it by cutting off the dollar. And the easiest thing you can do is educate others with what you've learned today. Go out and tell someone about the child sex slavery in Thailand. Tell them about the rape and the sexual exploitation. It's a horrible subject to talk about but once they are informed they can make a difference too.

Now the loss of a child is something in our culture that is becoming a standpoint [common]. We see it on the news every night but it's not something that should be tolerated. And a horrible image and a horrible reality is if we remember our childhood and see friends, cousins, nephews, or any other relatives and, god forbid, our own children being taken away from us in the middle of the night, forced into this type of exploitation, chained to a bed for the rest of their lives to be raped everyday of their existence. Now this is an image we would not wish on anyone to become real. But it's real for too many families in Thailand right now. Now that you know what's going on and how to do it, you too can stop this ultimate evil from happening again. Thank you.

SPEECH EVALUATION FORM

SPEAKER Chris Jowers   **TOPIC** "Child Sex Slavery in Thailand"   **DATE** _____

Overall Considerations

5	Did the speaker seem committed to the topic?
5	Did the speech meet the requirements of the assignment?
4	Was the speech adapted to fit the audience?
4	Did the speech promote identification among topic, audience, and speaker?
4	Was the purpose of the speech clear?
4	Was the topic handled with imagination and freshness?
4	Did the speech meet high ethical standards?

Substance

5	Was the topic worthwhile?
4	Had the speaker done sufficient research?
4	Were the main ideas supported with reliable and relevant information?
4	Was testimony used appropriately?
3	Were the sources documented appropriately?
2	Were examples or narratives used effectively?
3	Was the reasoning clear and correct?

Structure

4	Did the introduction spark your interest?
5	Did the introduction adequately preview the message?
4	Was the speech easy to follow?
4	Could you identify the main points of the speech?
4	Were transitions used to tie the speech together?
4	Did the conclusion summarize the message?
5	Did the conclusion help you remember the speech?

Presentation

5	Was the language clear, simple, and direct?
5	Was the language colorful?
5	Were grammar and pronunciations correct?
5	Was the speech presented extemporaneously?
5	Were notes used unobtrusively?
5	Was the speaker appropriately enthusiastic?
5	Did the speaker maintain good eye contact?
4	Did gestures and body language complement ideas?
5	Was the speaker's voice expressive?
5	Were the rate and loudness appropriate to the material?
5	Did the speaker uses pauses appropriately?
4	Did presentation aids make the message clearer or more memorable?
4	Were presentation aids skillfully integrated into the speech?
5	Was the presentation free from distracting mannerisms?

Discussion Guide for "Child Sex Slavery in Thailand"

1. What is the structural design of Chris Jower's persuasive speech?

2. What special problems did Chris have to confront in adapting this topic to his audience?

3. Does Chris come across as a credible communicator on this problem? Why or why not?

4. What are Chris's strengths as a persuader? In what areas does he need to improve?

Commentary on "Child Sex Slavery in Thailand"

Chris Jowers selected his topic because ". . . it was a subject that I felt needed to be out there in the public eye." He wanted to make a difference, he said, "even in such a small way." The topic called for a classic problem-solution persuasive speech.

Because the problem was little known, he had to make his audience aware of it. Compounding the ignorance of his listeners was their probable indifference. What would his audience of college students in Memphis care about a problem so far away from their everyday lives?

This twin rhetorical challenge of overcoming ignorance and indifference was large enough, we feel, that Chris should have spent more time upon it, even if it meant he would have to summarize more quickly his recommendations for audience action. Chris does offer a graphic general description of the fate of affected children and some statistics concerning the overall magnitude of the problem. But these descriptions and the claims based upon them are so sensational that some critical listeners would be apt to dismiss them as hyperbole and to accuse Chris of adopting a kind of "tabloid style" of description. A general rule holds true again: *The more sensational the claim, the more the persuader must present careful documentation from respected sources of information.* Chris needed more such documentation, preferably from sources less biased perhaps than the activist organizations he mentions. He also needed more specific examples and stories of real, not just hypothetical, cases to convey an undeniable sense of this human tragedy.

In developing the motivating section of his speech, "why you should take action," Chris needs to state his reasons more clearly. Inexactitude of language and thought is a special problem in this speech. Not only does vagueness create confusion, it also raises questions of competence. When Chris tells his listeners in Memphis they can make a difference even though they are "a thousand miles away" from Thailand, critical listeners are apt to raise an eyebrow at such carelessness of expression. When Chris warns that the problem is spreading throughout Asia, and that "America may be next," they may find the claim outlandish and wonder if Chris is not indulging in the "slippery slope" fallacy described in Chapter 14. In short, they may well wonder whether they can depend on Chris as a trustworthy source of information and advice, and even wonder at the entire validity of the real problem he wishes so earnestly to affect. On the other hand, he must not abandon his direct, extemporaneous style of presentation to achieve this greater precision of expression. But he should dress more nicely to suggest that he thinks this speech is a special occasion and to affirm his seriousness. He must portray himself as a mature, as well as a sincere, advocate.

We like the passion and commitment Chris reveals on this issue and are impressed with the research effort he has made. He demonstrates a proper persuader's attitude: he would like to have some impact on reality and to change the course of events through his words. We would assign his effort a "B" grade.

Assisted Suicide: A Person's Right to Die

David A. Pojman

As you remember, I am a nursing student here at the University of Memphis. As you saw by the previous speech, there are many good reasons that assisted suicide should not be legalized. Now I would like to tell you why I think that assisted suicide should be legalized.

In 1988 Dr. Jack Kevorkian helped his first terminally ill client to die. This act was greeted with **much** dismay and anger in the medical community and it intensified the debate over a very **difficult** question: Should a terminally ill person be allowed to die when other palliative measures have failed to ease that person's suffering? Assisted suicide not only is an important issue in the medical community, it also has become an important issue in public debate, not only in the United States but all over the world. Assisted suicide is defined as a person providing a substance or device capable of causing death with the full knowledge that that person intends to use it to cause their own death.

Should assisted suicide be legalized? I think it should be and there are five reasons I have for this. They include the issue of a person suffering, the person's right to self-determination, an economic argument, a religious argument, and also Dr. Jack Kevorkian's impact on assisted suicide.

First let's take a look at the suffering issue. The National Center for Health Statistics estimate that seven hundred and fifty thousand Americans die each year of diseases capable of causing excruciating pain. These diseases include cancer, AIDS, lung and liver disease. The experts say that pain with these patients can be controlled ninety percent of the time but this leaves seventy-five thousand individuals to die each year with uncontrollable pain. In advanced-stage cancer patients seventy percent of them say they suffer pain. Of that seventy percent, nine out of ten categorize their pain as severe.

The support for the issue of the suffering client was best presented by Stewart Alsop, a respected journalist who died in 1975 of cancer. Alsop was a patient in the hospital and he had a roommate named Jack. Jack was twenty eight years old, had terminal cancer, and was very close to death. When Alsop was in the hospital he kept a journal of all his days there and this is what he wrote about Jack and Jack's suffering. "At the prescribed hour a nurse would give Jack a shot of the synthetic analgesic and this would control the pain for perhaps two hours. Then he would begin to moan or whimper very low as though he didn't want to wake me. And then he would begin to howl like a dog." This went on for three days and again Alsop wrote a entry into his journal that sums up the belief of the suffering argument: "The third night of this routine the terrible thought occurred to me. If Jack were a dog, what would be done for him? The answer was obvious—the pound and chloroform. No human being with a spark of pity could let a living thing suffer so to no good end." As can be seen by this story, there is no question that some terminally ill people suffer terrible pain. Faced with such a dilemma, many people would understand a person's desire to commit assisted suicide.

A second argument supporting assisted suicide is a client's right to self-determination. The supporters of self determination believe it is ultimately the person's right to choose their own destiny. A person has the right through the use of living wills or durable powers of attorney to name someone to make decisions for them, should they become incompetent. The question I pose to you is this: If a client can decide who makes their decisions when they become incompetent, why are they not able to decide while still competent about carrying out their own death? In 1981, the Supreme Court stated, "No right is more sacred or is more carefully guarded than the right of the individual to possession and control of their own person."

The economic argument is the third view supporting assisted suicide I'd like to talk about. In 1991 five hundred and fourteen thousand people died of cancer. The costs for the medical care of these individuals in the last years of their life was eighteen billion dollars. This is fifty one percent of the total money that was spent to treat cancer in 1991. This is an astronomical figure that shows the costs client and insurance companies must endure. Also, in this day and age many people do not have the means or the insurance to pay for these costs. Thus, the burden is put on the taxpayers of the United States.

Another argument supporting assisted suicide is the view of religion. In 1991, a survey done by the Partridge Center found that all major United States denominations encourage the practice of allowing a terminally ill patient to die through the withholding or withdrawing of medical treatment. Also, holy books such as the Bible and the Koran do not prohibit or specifically address euthanasia in any form.

Finally I would like to address Dr. Jack Kevorkian and his impact on assisted suicide. Dr. Kevorkian is the reason assisted suicide should be legalized. He sometimes uses inhumane methods to perform assisted suicide. An example of this is carbon monoxide. This is not a peaceful death. The person will experience difficulty breathing, confusion, and develop a severe headache before succumbing to the effects of the gas. Dr. Kevorkian's vigilante style of assisted suicide is unacceptable and needs to be stopped. If legalized, inhumane methods such as using carbon monoxide would be made illegal.

As can be seen, there are some very compelling views supporting assisted suicide. In the last two months two federal appeals courts have overturned rulings that would have stopped assisted suicides. These courts in California and New York have begun what is surely to be a process that will eventually lead to the legalization of assisted suicide. I believe it should be legalized. Today in America everything we do is based on rights we have as citizens. These rights include the right to life, the right to privacy, and the right to free speech. So why doesn't a person have the right to die? I believe it is ultimately the person's right to choose to die as long as they are found competent to make that decision. Thank you. Can I answer any questions?

SPEECH EVALUATION FORM

SPEAKER David A. Pojman   **TOPIC** "Assisted Suicide: A Person's Right to Die"   **DATE** _____

Overall Considerations

5	Did the speaker seem committed to the topic?
5	Did the speech meet the requirements of the assignment?
3	Was the speech adapted to fit the audience?
3	Did the speech promote identification among topic, audience, and speaker?
5	Was the purpose of the speech clear?
3	Was the topic handled with imagination and freshness?
5	Did the speech meet high ethical standards?

Substance

5	Was the topic worthwhile?
5	Had the speaker done sufficient research?
4	Were the main ideas supported with reliable and relevant information?
4	Was testimony used appropriately?
4	Were the sources documented appropriately?
4	Were examples or narratives used effectively?
3	Was the reasoning clear and correct?

Structure

2	Did the introduction spark your interest?
4	Did the introduction adequately preview the message?
4	Was the speech easy to follow?
4	Could you identify the main points of the speech?
2	Were transitions used to tie the speech together?
1	Did the conclusion summarize the message?
2	Did the conclusion help you remember the speech?

Presentation

5	Was the language clear, simple, and direct?
2	Was the language colorful?
5	Were grammar and pronunciations correct?
2	Was the speech presented extemporaneously?
1	Were notes used unobtrusively?
2	Was the speaker appropriately enthusiastic?
2	Did the speaker maintain good eye contact?
2	Did gestures and body language complement ideas?
1	Was the speaker's voice expressive?
3	Were the rate and loudness appropriate to the material?
3	Did the speaker uses pauses appropriately?
NA	Did presentation aids make the message clearer or more memorable?
NA	Were presentation aids skillfully integrated into the speech?
4	Was the presentation free from distracting mannerisms?

Discussion Guide for "Assisted Suicide: A Person's Right to Die"

1. How skillfully does David weave the fabric of evidence, proof, and argument that we discuss in Chapter 14? What specific suggestions for improvement would you make to him?

2. What strands of deductive and inductive reasoning did you find in David's case?

3. How effectively does he use internal summaries and transitions?

4. Is David an effective advocate of his point of view? How might he make a better presentation?

Commentary on "Assisted Suicide: A Person's Right to Die"

David Pojman's persuasive speech helps us understand the dynamics we discuss in Chapter 14 of building an argument on one side of a controversial issue. David establishes personal ethos in his opening by reminding listeners that he is a nursing student and gracefully acknowledges a previous speech that presents the other side of the argument. He states the critical question of the controversy, defines important terms in the dispute, and announces the position he will defend. Thereafter, things begin to unravel as David attempts to weave a fabric of evidence, proof, and argument.

One immediate problem is that David needs to state his main points far more forcefully. Instead of saying, for example, "let's look at the economic argument," David should say, "When we defy the wishes of hopelessly ill people and prolong their lives, we waste an incredible amount of money." Another problem is that he tries to develop too many main points for such a short speech. Most of these points seem rather anemic and embryonic.

His best developed main point is his first one concerning patient suffering. He uses both statistical and narrative forms of evidence to support this point, and in the process demonstrates that he has done responsible research. Both the statistics and the illustrative story give his speech a sound inductive base: his argument seems grounded in reality. It is not, however, without logical flaw. The fact that pain can be controlled only ninety percent of the time in terminal cases does not entail the conclusion that ten percent of terminal patients must therefore die in excruciating pain. As he states the statistics, they could just as easily mean that *all* such patients may go through unrelieved pain an average ten percent of the time during their illnesses. He invokes a good basic principle to argue from, but once again, he needs to state the point more emphatically, such as "No one should have to suffer excruciating pain needlessly." Even in implicit form, this principle gives his argument a strong deductive leg to stand on.

The pathos of the Alsop story should surely evoke more emotion in the telling of it, but David's speech is handicapped throughout by his absolutely colorless presentation. He needs to escape from his notes, establish a good sense of communication with listeners, and use pause to reinforce his points. He needs a more expressive face and manner to convey the power of his convictions.

As he moves on to his point concerning self-determination, David argues well by analogy that if we grant the right to a living will, we should also grant the right of a competent person to request assisted suicide. The word "competent" is important here, because it serves to qualify David's argument. The point, however, ends rather abruptly without further explanation. David needs an internal summary both to focus the importance of what he has demonstrated and to form a transition to his next point.

His economic point is also badly truncated. Having pointed out the high cost of caring for terminally-ill cancer patients during their last years, David needed to draw the inference for listeners and to complete the unit of proof. For example, he might have concluded that this money was wasted when prolonged treatment was not wanted by patients, and that it might have been much better spent on research for preventions and cures. Similarly, he needed to conclude his religion point by drawing inferences in support of his case. Once again he also needed to develop an internal summary and transition moving into his final point.

His indictment of Dr. Kevorkian gives his argument a surprising turn. But he needed to conclude with a more powerful summary before moving to his final reflections.

In short, David had done good research for this speech, introduced it well, and obviously cared a great deal about the issue. He needs, however, to develop more skill in weaving and presenting persuasive arguments. We would assign this speech a "B–" grade.

On the Preservation of the Ozone

Tanvir Hossain

How many of you knew what the word "ozone" meant ten years ago? To tell you the truth myself, I didn't even know what the word ozone meant. Now the word is being used like a household name. In simplest terms, in 1991 *Science* magazine said the definition of the ozone is an outer sphere of the earth that protects the earth from poisonous gases that are artificially altered into the environment, mainly from big companies. The ozone also blocks out ultraviolet rays which produce smog and can raise the earth's temperature. The problem with the ozone layer today is that it is disappearing at a very fast rate due to the fact that people are misusing the environment for their own self-interest and not keeping their future interest in mind. *Science News* of 1994 explains how the preservation of the ozone can be achieved if people have just some general knowledge of it and if they were willing to sacrifice a few of their commodities of their everyday life.

Today I'm here to persuade you to help preserve the ozone so you and your children in the future can enjoy life by giving you some important facts about the ozone, some causes and problems that contribute to the ozone depletion today, and some key steps that individuals like you yourself can take to help preserve the ozone. Nearly two decades ago the word ozone was probably not in a lot of peoples' vocabulary. There were no problems until the Environmental Protection Agency discovered a large hole in the ozone in Anarctica during the early 1980s. Since then the later part of the 1980s has experienced six of the hottest temperature increases in the earth's recorded history. Terms like "global warming" came into perspective and the word was being printed in international relations books and the meaning of it is the prospective climate change that the insulating effect of the earth's atmosphere may cause. Greenhouse gases such as CO_2 and CFL were being artificially inseminated by freon in refrigerators and air conditioners of course. And these gases are eating up the ozone layer today. According to the *Human Health Survey and Service Report* of 1996, it is projected that the temperature of the earth will rise up four degrees by the year 2050. With that in mind this leads me to some of the main factors that are destroying the ozone layer today.

Deforestation is one of the main factors. The ozone is disappearing, according to the Environmental Protection Agency, because rain forests are being massacred left and right. Deforestation accounts for twenty-five percent of excess CO_2. Governments and large corporations are tearing down forests in places like Asia, Africa, and large parts of South America. According to a national consensus the Environmental Protection Agency took in 1992, for every twenty-four seconds, rain forests of the equivalent of six football fields are being destroyed. That's quite a bit. According to the article in 1996 in *Greenpeace*, E. I. DuPont de Nemours and Company Incorporated is one of the leading causes of creating CFL, which also is one of the leading causes of ozone depletion in the world. *Greenpeace* says, "Corporations serve their own interests without keeping the preservation of the environment in mind." You'll never hear about these facts because large corporations that damage the environment hire their own omissions testers to cover up their exploitation.

These problems can cause some short- and long-term effects. DHH made a report in 1995 that a short-term problem is heavy smog, which is basically created in large crowded cities and it contributes a lot to air pollution. The American Lung Association has tied this with several cases of people having trouble breathing and has also acquired this to lung cancer. They have tied it in. A long-term effect would be the rise in temperature. Most people will have a general stigma presently that [when] the ozone is gone [then] they're going to burn up in the areas where there are big gaps. *Time* magazine wrote an article in 1995 giving us some more realistic effects that we can probably be looking forward to in the future. Rising temperatures can create ultraviolet rays of course, but they will ruin hundred of thousands of crops. What this means is that the population of the world will increase from five billion to five-point-five billion by the year 2000 and without relying on a lot of crops that we need for food—we're not going to have it. The worldwide issue will be the preservation of food. Another long-term factor will be the rise of water from the oceans due, of course, to the rise in temperatures. The article explains that most of the coastal cities in the world will probably be under water. Just imagine having, going to Atlanta and picturing a beach over there and snorkeling out in Florida. That's kind of scary.

However, there are some steps you can take to help preserve the ozone layer for you and for future generations. Write to your local congressmen in areas where a lot of rain forests are being depleted. And speak out against that. Cut down on products such as deodorant sprays, hairsprays, and avoid buying any refrigerators that contain freon. Also try to use air conditioners only when necessary. As opposed to using deodorant sprays an alternative can be deodorant sticks. Because that will cut down on a large portion of gases that deplete the ozone today. Also recycle products like cans and bottles and in turn buy recycled products. Most importantly, take the time to learn about the ozone because it is really not the government's responsibility to take care of our earth, but it is our own.

Today I hope I have persuaded you to act in regards to helping preserve our ozone. I have told you some general information about the ozone, some current causes, and problems that are contributing to ozone depletion today and some steps you too can take to help preserve our ozone for us and for future generations. Right now I am going to hand out some other steps that you can take and, by the way, these papers are recycled.

SPEECH EVALUATION FORM

SPEAKER Tanvir Hossain   **TOPIC** "On the Preservation of the Ozone"   **DATE** _____

Overall Considerations

3	Did the speaker seem committed to the topic?
2	Did the speech meet the requirements of the assignment?
3	Was the speech adapted to fit the audience?
2	Did the speech promote identification among topic, audience, and speaker?
4	Was the purpose of the speech clear?
2	Was the topic handled with imagination and freshness?
3	Did the speech meet high ethical standards?

Substance

5	Was the topic worthwhile?
3	Had the speaker done sufficient research?
3	Were the main ideas supported with reliable and relevant information?
4	Was testimony used appropriately?
4	Were the sources documented appropriately?
3	Were examples or narratives used effectively?
3	Was the reasoning clear and correct?

Structure

2	Did the introduction spark your interest?
4	Did the introduction adequately preview the message?
3	Was the speech easy to follow?
2	Could you identify the main points of the speech?
2	Were transitions used to tie the speech together?
4	Did the conclusion summarize the message?
2	Did the conclusion help you remember the speech?

Presentation

1	Was the language clear, simple, and direct?
3	Was the language colorful?
1	Were grammar and pronunciations correct?
1	Was the speech presented extemporaneously?
1	Were notes used unobtrusively?
3	Was the speaker appropriately enthusiastic?
2	Did the speaker maintain good eye contact?
2	Did gestures and body language complement ideas?
3	Was the speaker's voice expressive?
3	Were the rate and loudness appropriate to the material?
2	Did the speaker uses pauses appropriately?
NA	Did presentation aids make the message clearer or more memorable?
NA	Were presentation aids skillfully integrated into the speech?
3	Was the presentation free from distracting mannerisms?

Discussion Guide for "On the Preservation of the Ozone"

1. How would you evaluate the research Tanvir did for this speech? Did it result in responsible knowledge?

2. Did Tanvir present a persuasive speech? Answer this question in light of the characteristics of persuasive speaking discussed in Chapter 13.

3. Discuss the design and structure of his speech. Is it effective? Does he use supporting materials well?

4. How effective is the language and presentation of this speech?

Commentary on "On the Preservation of the Ozone"

Tanvir Hossain's speech raises a number of instructive questions concerning the nature of responsible knowledge, structuring and supporting persuasive speeches, adapting to an audience, and presentation.

To prepare for his speech on preserving the ozone, Tanvir did a considerable amount of research. However, time spent in the library does not necessarily equate with responsible knowledge. Tanvir does not acknowledge that the fate of the ozone layer is a controversial issue pitting experts against each other. Is global warming real, and is it the result of human exploitation of the environment? How much of a threat is it, and how valid are such projections that the sea will soon engulf lowlying coastal areas? Scientists disagree, and critical listeners are apt to suspect any speech that does not report this disagreement faithfully. Tanvir could have acknowledged this controversy and still posed this critical question: Can we afford to be wrong on this issue? Must we not proceed on the assumption that global warming and ozone depletion are real problems, and that these might dramatically alter the environment unless we are more responsible custodians?

Tanvir was assigned to give a persuasive speech, but considering the characteristics of persuasion discussed in Chapter 13, one might well conclude that he presented an informative speech with a few recommendations tacked on. He needed a more effective introduction that would tie the topic more compellingly to his life and to his listeners' vital interests: the closely-related speech offered at the end of Chapter 8 in *Public Speaking* shows how these relationships can be established. He does state his purpose clearly, and previews his speech. It appears to follow a problem-solution pattern, but the problem phase of it lacks clear structure. For example, it is difficult to determine where his point on deforestation ends and what precisely follows it. Not only should he state subpoints more clearly, he also should develop transitions that tie them together. Moreover, he could pause to signal the move from one point to another. This lack of clear structure and focus discourages the understanding phase of the persuasive process. As he transforms his research into supporting materials, Tanvir should not cite biased sources on controversial claims. DuPont may well be responsible for much damage to the environment, but critical listeners might decide that Greenpeace is not an unbiased source for such allegations. He does develop an adequate conclusion that summarizes his speech and offers a handout to reinforce its meaning.

Some of Tanvir's recommendations seem quite valid, but others raise questions of credibility. One such recommendation, that we should write our "congressmen in the area of rain forests," not only uses sexist language but seems strange, given the fact that there are no such rain forests in the continental United States. Even if there were, Tanvir should specify the government officials his particular audience should write, and give their addresses. This would signify a more precise adaptation to his immediate audience. Finally, some recommendations may not be relevant to contemporary conditions. When Tanvir tells us not to use deodorant or hair sprays and to avoid purchasing appliances that use freon, he needs to acknowledge recent laws that have made such sprays more safe and transformed the chemical composition of refrigerants used in new appliances. Not to indicate his knowledge of such changes is to risk an overall impression that his speech lacks a foundation of responsible knowledge.

The most obvious problem in this speech is that it is not really presented. Rather, it is for the most part read, and not very well at that. Tanvir needed to rehearse his presentation so that he could relate directly to his listeners. We know that he is capable of more effective communication: When he uses the excellent analogy comparing the size of lost forestlands to "six football fields every twenty-four seconds," Tanvir exclaims "That's quite a bit!" Indeed, and that is a glimmer of the kind of direct communication with an audience that Tanvir needs to cultivate as he develops extemporaneous skills. As he concludes his speech and offers his handout, he notes with wry humor that it is printed on recycled paper. This was a nice touch, and holds the promise for his developing better communication skills.

We would encourage the question-answer period he invites at the end of his speech. Often students like Tanvir, as they relax and answer questions directly, become their own models for improvement. We have often told such students, "See, you can do it! Now let's get these same qualities of conversational speaking into your next speech." We would also counsel Tanvir to be more careful of malapropisms: using "national consensus" when he apparently means "survey," "general stigma" when he seems to mean "erroneous impression," and describing freon's effect on the environment as "artificial insemination" are but three among many examples of questionable word choice.

We like the research effort in this speech, but in light of its various flaws, we would assign it a "D+" and challenge Tanvir to improve.